Uniquely **Bivocational**

Understanding the Life of a Pastor who has a Second Job

RAY GILDER

For Bivocational Pastors and Their Churches

salt & light
PUBLISHING

A Division of Publishers Solution

Uniquely **Bivocational**

By Ray Gilder
©2013 Ray Gilder. All rights reserved.

ISBN: 978-1-937925-10-9

Published By:

A Division of Publishers Solution

14805 Forest Rd., Suite 205
Forest, VA 24551
www.PublishersSolution.com

Cover & Interior Design by Heather Kirk, GraphicsForSuccess.com
Cover Photography of man in suit by Heather Kirk, GraphicsForSuccess.com
Cover Photography of Aerial View of Fields by Kevin Tuck, RGBstock.com

A Note From the Author

began to pray a specific prayer as I approached my fiftieth birthday. At that time, I was serving as the Church and Community Ministries Director for the Tennessee Baptist Convention. I enjoyed what I was doing but felt some frustration over being responsible for about a dozen different ministries in the state which kept me very busy moving from one thing to the next, but never allowed me time for closure on any one thing. I told someone that I felt like I got off my horse and went in twelve different directions every day. As I examined my life and realized I was about two-thirds through my ministry years, I began to pray: "Lord, I want to use the rest of my life doing something that will meet a need and make a difference."

In 1995, I was given the opportunity to lead the Tennessee Baptist Convention in ministering to the large number of bivocational pastors in the state. Throughout Tennessee and across the Southern Baptist Convention, bivocational pastors had practically been ignored and overlooked because most of them did not have the time to be as involved as their fully-funded preacher brothers. As I began to relate to and encourage these great men of God, I became aware that they were indeed choice servants of our Lord. An underlying goal I have had since beginning this ministry has been to raise the level of awareness and appreciation for the work of bivocational pastors in the Kingdom of God.

Since 2005, I have enjoyed the additional privilege of serving as National Coordinator of the Bivocational and Small Church Leadership Network. Through this opportunity I have developed an even deeper appreciation for the thousands of men who serve churches throughout the United States as bivocational pastors.

There are few books about bivocational ministry available today. The number of churches served by bivocational pastors is quite large. From everything I can see, that number will continue to increase every year.

A few months ago, I was approached by a dear friend, Dr. Jere Phillips, professor at Mid-America Baptist Theological Seminary. He was my supervisor at the Tennessee Baptist Convention when I was given the opportunity to work with bivocational pastors. He told me that I should write a book about bivocational ministry. Dr. Phillips has one of the sharpest minds of anyone I have ever met. I took his advice and felt God's leading in preparing the material for the book before you.

From the start, I have had two basic guidelines. I wanted it to be an easy read and I wanted it to be very practical. As you read this little book, I trust you will find both of these to be true.

I want to express gratitude to my dear wife, Diane, for typing and offering practical advice about text and content. I want to thank Dr. Jere Phillips for providing the initial challenge to put this book in print. I want to thank Dan Reber for volunteering to be responsible for taking the rough draft and getting it ready to print. I thank Bill and Nancy James for editing and formatting the text.

I thank the thousands of bivocational pastors who inspired me to champion their work in the Kingdom of God. Finally and most of all, I thank my Lord who counted me faithful and put me in the ministry of the Gospel.

Foreword

Nearly half of all churches are served by bivocational ministers. If underfunded pastors were included (those ministers
who depend on a wife's employment to support the family), the
percentage would be even greater. These men are not part-time
preachers, but serve their churches with their whole hearts and,
at the same time, diligently work at a second job, usually secular,
in order to support their families. Without the sacrifice of these
gallant ministers, thousands of churches would be unable to have a
vocational minister.

Bivocational ministers serve honorably and faithfully, although
they often go unrecognized in the shadow of larger ministries. These
servants of God are humble, not craving the spotlight or demanding
attention. Yet, they deserve our attention! We owe them respect
and support. Because many of these ministers have been unable
to pursue formal ministerial education, a major aspect of support
involves encouragement and training. While many volumes fill
the shelf of Christian bookstores regarding the general issues of
pastoral ministries, counseling, administration, evangelism, church
growth, and other issues, few approach these tasks from the unique
viewpoints of the bivocational minister.

Into this gap walks one of America's most effective leaders, a
man who understands and loves bivocational ministers; a man

who has walked where they walked, served where they serve, and lived where they live. Ray Gilder has earned a place among those modern giants of bivocational studies: Bill Neptune, Luther Dorr, Dale Holloway, Leon Wilson and Doran McCarty.

This book mirrors Ray Gilder's easy-to-listen-to style. His personal touch can be seen on each page. These pages are full of practical advice and personal examples.

Every bivocational minister (and every pastor and church member, for that matter) would benefit from this book. Don't just read it. Take it to heart and live it out. You'll walk away stronger and more blessed than when you picked it up to read it.

Jere Phillips, Ph.D.

Professor, Practical Theology
Mid-America Baptist Theological Seminary

Table of Contents

Introduction

Everyone has his own idea of what a pastor should be. If a survey were taken of the average church membership regarding their expectations of a pastor, even the Apostle Paul would fail to qualify. If this is true of the fully-funded pastor, how much more difficult it is for the bivocational pastor!

John struggled with feelings of inadequacy and insignificance. The concern he shared with me was the belief that someone else could do a better job than he was doing at his church. The demands of his second job and the need to be there for his family left him with insufficient time to do all he would like to do with his church. I reminded him that the church he pastored could not afford a fully-funded pastor. Whoever they had would have to have a second job. Secondly, even though he could not do all he would like to do, the church was better off with him as pastor than not have a pastor at all. This story could be repeated a thousand times or more as other bivo pastors have shared from their hearts. This book is an attempt to help my bivo pastor brothers realize that their labor is not in vain. God takes our little and does more than we realize.

Two key factors that keep a bivo pastor going are the call of God upon his life and the God-given desire to make a difference, whatever it takes. What was said of the priests in the Old Testament is true of pastors today: *"And no man taketh this honor upon himself, but he that is called of God, as was Aaron."* (Hebrews 5:4). Knowing that God has called him elevates a pastor's motivation and accountability beyond the opinions and actions of man. A pastor knows that he will one day give an account to God. *"Obey them that have the rule over you, and submit yourselves: for they watch for your souls, as they must give account, that they may do it with joy, not with grief: for that is unprofitable for you"* (Hebrews 13:17).

The bivo pastor is driven by a desire to make a difference. He may not be the best pastor, preach the greatest sermons, or build the biggest church, but his desire is to *"by all means save some"* as the Apostle Paul stated about his ministry. *"To the weak became I as weak, that I might gain the weak: I am made all things to all men that I might by all means save some."* (I Corinthians 9:22).

The number of bivo pastors is growing across North America. It is my belief that church leadership of the future will be primarily bivocational. This book is an attempt to encourage, strengthen, validate, and challenge bivocational leaders in the work God has given them to do.

Chapter 1

What's in a Name?

What in the world is a "bivocational" pastor? Most everyone has a basic understanding of "pastor." It is the word "bivocational" which raises questions. Simply put, the word refers to a pastor who has two vocations. The root meaning of vocation is "calling." A bivocational pastor is called to pastor a church and also has another job or activity to which he gives part of his time and attention. Both vocations may be ministry related. For example, the past seventeen years I have pastored a church and been employed by the Tennessee Baptist Convention. For the last six years I have been tri-vocational, additionally serving as National Coordinator of the Bivocational and Small Church Leadership Network.

For the bivo pastor, the second vocation may be full or part-time. This means that some of his time is spent in matters other than pastoral work. Student pastors should be considered bivocational because of the demands of their studies. Even a retired person who serves as pastor is usually looked upon as bivocational because all of his funding does not come from the church.

Bivocational Pastor—Not Bivocational Church

There is no such thing as a bivocational church. There are churches which are led by bivocational pastors, but no church has two vocations. The church which is led by a bivo pastor is not "part-time" if it has regular services and activities each week. A part-time church is one which meets only once or twice a month.

A bivo pastor is not a "part-time" pastor. He may be receiving part-time pay, but if he is the pastor, he is pastor all the time. He may not be able to respond immediately to a crisis but he carries the responsibility to pastor his congregation.

Why Single Out Bivo Pastors?

Some may question why pastors are divided into two groups—fully-funded and bivocational. Those of us who seek to encourage and support bivocational pastors did not create the division. It was already there. We realized that bivo pastors usually cannot attend Monday morning pastors' meetings and most other mid-week events because they have a scheduling conflict with more than one vocation.

Instead of ignoring them because they cannot attend the regular meetings, leaders need to make every attempt to work with them when they can be available. Bivo pastors have many unique needs, which will be fully addressed later, such as learning how to manage their time well, balancing family and church responsibilities, finding time to get the necessary training, and meeting the demands of a second and usually full-time job.

Why Use the Term "Bivocational"?

Many terms have been used to describe bivocational pastors. Some call them double-duty ministers, dual career ministers, or working preachers or tentmakers. After spending several years studying the subject, those of us who provide leadership for the Bivocational and Small Church Leadership Network have determined that "bivocational" is probably the best term and decided to use it consistently in order to eliminate as much confusion as possible. Though sometimes written with a hyphen, as suggested by "spell check" the preferable spelling is bivocational, not bi-vocational.   According to some experts, either spelling is acceptable. This unhyphenated version has been in use for almost twenty years and is the preferred spelling. As an aside, it is interesting to note that "spell check" does not recognize "pastored" or "pastoring" either.

Not everyone agrees with or understands what "bivocational" means. Several years ago I was speaking at a church in the absence of their pastor. I asked the members if their pastor was bivocational and was told that he was not. I then asked "Where is he?" Their reply was "He's at work!"

Times Are Changing

In early America most pastors were bivocational. Usually they were either a pastor-school teacher or a pastor-farmer. During the extensive church growth period after World War II, the Southern Baptist Convention made a push for every church to have a fully-funded pastor and provide a home for him and his family. Soon the attitude developed that if a pastor had another job, he was a second rate preacher who was not capable of serving a fully-funded church. In the last ten to fifteen years, however, the awareness and appreciation for bivocational ministry has been on the increase. Bivocational pastors, as well as other bivocational ministry staff, are becoming much more comfortable with their roles. Because of the downturn in the economy, more and more churches are hiring a bivocational staff. Today bivocational ministry is being looked upon as the wave of the future.

Chapter 2

Should Any Pastor be Bivocational?

Some well-meaning leaders think that no pastor should ever be bivocational. This thought may stem from arrogance and prejudice but also from a lack of understanding of the times in which we live. If this is a genuine expression of how many people feel, then we should deal with the question sincerely, carefully and very thoughtfully.

Again, "Should any pastor be bivocational?" What would prompt that question? What is really being said? Some may say that if a bivo pastor had enough faith, he would just quit his job and trust God to meet his needs? Many have suggested that the bivo pastor needs to start "living by faith." Well, if God chooses to meet his needs through another job rather than through an increase in the church budget, that is His business. Success in ministry is not always labeled "fully-funded." Years ago, a bivo pastor shared with me his struggle in this area. He was driving down the road praying about quitting his job and going full-time at the church. As he drove by a river he decided to stop the car and go stand on the bank of the river. On a whim he stepped into the water. Instead of walking on the water, he sank to his waist. He looked up and said "Lord, why can't I walk on the water? Peter did." Then came the Lord's reply "But I told him to do it."

Others may remark to the bivo pastor "if you were a good enough preacher, you could get a bigger church." This is an arrogant assumption. It indicates the conclusion that those who cannot preach, get small churches, and those who can, get bigger churches. It has been my experience that some very powerful preachers are serving smaller churches. By the same token, there are some not so powerful preachers in larger churches. Sometimes church growth takes place when a church is led by a pastor who is not a great preacher, but has great administrative skills, excellent people skills and the wisdom to put the right people in leadership positions. We all need to realize that God places His men where He wants them to be, and if they are doing His business—He is "calling the shots!"

Some believe that a small congregation does not deserve to be called a church? Why did Jesus say *where two or three are gathered together in my name, there am I in the midst of them?* (Matthew 18:20). The Christian movement started in house churches and many are predicting that it will end in the same place. The number of people in attendance does not establish the validity of a church. The real test is: Is the Spirit of God present?

Some are of the opinion a church is not a real church if it does not have a full menu of activities. When a church is growing, other pastors will ask about the programs the church is using; and then try to copy them. Years ago I heard of a pastor of a large church in North Carolina who was asked, "What kind of youth program do you have?" He answered, "Preaching, praying, singing and shouting!" He was asked "What kind of children's program do you have?" His answer was "Preaching, praying, singing and shouting!" Many churches and pastors are guilty of copying the latest "fad" that is said to be attracting crowds. The church can no longer compete with the world in providing entertainment. Each church is unique and must find out what the Lord wants it to do—and do it well!

Some question whether over half of the pastors in the Southern Baptist Convention are out of God's will because they are bivocational? In many parts of North America, churches with two hundred in attendance are considered to be large. Many small and rural communities in this country are thankful for a man who will work another job so they can have a pastor. Why do we applaud a man who plants his life in an obscure place in a foreign country but ignore one who does that in our own country?

There are many reasons why a man would become a bivocational pastor. Some are inspired by the Apostle Paul. Paul supported himself by making tents while he focused on preaching the Gospel and starting churches. *"And because he was of the same craft, he abode with them, and wrought: for by their occupation they were tentmakers"* (Acts 18:3). He refused to be a financial burden to others. *"For yourselves know how ye ought to follow us: for we behaved not ourselves* disorderly among you; Neither did we eat any man's bread for nought; but wrought with labor and travail night and day, that we might not be chargeable to any of you: Not because we have not power, but to make ourselves an ensample unto you to follow us. " (II Thessalonians 3:7-9). It appears Paul did a pretty good job ministering for the Lord even though he was bivocational.

Many men are called to work another job so that a smaller membership church can have a pastor. Over half of all Southern Baptist Churches in America have fifty or less in Sunday school. Many of these churches could not continue without men who are willing to support their families through a second vocation. These men deserve accolades, not accusations of having no faith.

The type man we are discussing will not view his church as a step to one that is "bigger and better." Do pastors who have proven themselves faithful in a smaller membership church ever get an opportunity to pastor a larger church? Absolutely! He should, however, always seek God's leadership before taking any church and go with the plan to plant his life there until God moves him. There is no move up when he is where God put him. But, it is interesting that seldom does anyone say he is being led to a smaller congregation!

I read several years ago that a pastor's most productive year at his church will be the seventh. If that's true, many pastors never experience their best results. Statistics show that the average length of most pastorates is three and one half years. It certainly is not God-honoring for so many pastors to be looking for bigger and better churches. It is easily documented that pastors who have the greatest impact on their communities are those who have long tenures.

A man who is willing to invest his life in a small church which may never be able to pay him a salary that will fully support his family is definitely a candidate for bivocational ministry. Many men get a taste of what it is like to be bivocational while in college or seminary, and then move out of that status as soon as possible. But the pastor who answers the call to a small church in a rural or difficult area realizes he may be bivocational for his entire ministry.

God calls men to go into the market places of the world to carry the light of the gospel. The pastor and his family may be the church for a while. The church may be a house church or a store front church, but he will be committed to planting a church in a community where there is little or no gospel witness. According to recent stats America is the third largest unchurched nation in the world. Until just a few years ago the plan for funding church planting in America was a three year commitment with decreasing funding each year in the hope that the church would be self-supporting at the end of that period. That plan was not very practical or successful. Even if the plan worked, there are not enough funds to send the thousands of workers necessary for the task. A minister who is working in the marketplace will have the opportunity to demonstrate the validity of Christianity and share the message of hope and salvation to a world of people who may never attend church until they meet Christ through personal witness. For the man who is called to this task, there may be little salary other than what he earns in another vocation.

Many men are intentionally bivocational and others are bivocational by default. When God calls a man into the ministry in later life and he has spent years training for and building a career, he can answer that call as an intentional bivocational pastor. I've discovered in my work with bivocationals that these account for a large number of bivocational pastors. There is another group. They are the ones who planned and trained for full time ministry but found that there was not a church available that could fully fund their family. Because they have no training in a field other than ministry, they are forced to take a low paying job or the wife goes to work to provide for the family. I believe this will be the case more and more in the future. How much better it would be for a young preacher to get a double major while he has the opportunity in order to have a marketable skill if he should need to supplement his salary from the church

I did not know forty-five years ago that I would be working with bivocational pastors across the country, but God did. He let me experience some of these situations in my ministry. I worked forty hours a week at a hardware store and pastored a small country church. My wife also worked and went to school. After graduation my home church asked me to come as their pastor. Because I was exhausted and broke I thought it would be a good idea to take a short break before going on to seminary so I agreed to take the church. The church had a congregation of approximately two hundred and was fully-funded. Our stay lasted over six years and two children. Then God moved us to a small country church with fewer than fifty people. During the three and one half years I was there, I taught school and worked at a grocery store. My good friends and family told me I had gotten out of God's will because that's not the way God works. I didn't know why God had done that either. But now forty-five years later, I know why. God answers most of our questions—but in His timing. I needed personal experience in order to understand what bivocational and small church pastors experience. God was sending me to His school to prepare me for the ministry I now have. My short break between college and seminary stretched into ten years, but they were years that God used.

Sometimes a pastor is bivocational so that his church may be able to invest more money in ministry and missions. The percentage of a church's budget that goes to staff salaries and benefits is significant. The smaller the church the greater the percentage required for staff. A church that is serviced by a bivocational pastor will have more money to invest in ministry and mission causes. One pastor in Kentucky whose church has several hundred in attendance told me a year ago they had decided all staff would become bivocational in order to put more money into ministry and missions. His statement was "we feel we can be just as effective as bivocational leaders!"

Interestingly, in the last several years a number of retired pastors who are now serving bivocationally in smaller churches have told me that if they could start all over, they would be intentionally bivocational for their entire ministry. So, should any pastor be bivocational? Definitely! Why be critical of a man who is willing to work double duty in order to provide for his family while giving pastoral leadership to a church that needs him?

Without a doubt, our Lord said *"well done"* to the Apostle Paul after he finished his work on earth. Without a doubt, He will say the same to many bivocational pastors and their families who have answered the call and been willing to serve in unsung places for the glory of God.

Chapter 3

The Need for Bivocational Pastors & Church Planters

One of the most startling discoveries when studying the make-up of churches in the United States is how many churches actually have fewer than one hundred in Sunday morning attendance. Dr. Kevin Ezell, President of the North American Mission Board, said that his greatest learning curve, when assuming his position was discovering the vast number of bivocational pastors in the Southern Baptist Convention. He said "not until I came to the North American Mission Board did I realize the enormity of what bivocational pastors do in North America."[1]

---

1 Baptist Press, Ezell: Bivocational Pastors are SBC's *"Iron Men"* by Mickey Noah, June 25, 2012

The LifeWay Research Team has provided us with a statistical chart of the attendance in Southern Baptist churches. That chart can be accessed by going to the Bivocational and Small Church Leadership Network web site bivosmallchurch.net. Then check the sideboard "SBC Stats." A simple synopsis given in general figures is: 25% of all SBC churches have 25 or less in Sunday School; 50% have 50 or less; 75% have 100 or less and 81% have 125 or less. Our definition of a smaller membership church is 125 or less in Sunday school. This amounts to around 37,000 churches. Most of these churches are led by bivocational pastors. The reality is that the income in a large majority of these churches is not adequate to cover basic budget expenditures and provide a reasonable salary for the pastor.

Declining Churches Seek Bivocational Pastors

Another factor which contributes to the need for bivocational pastors is the decline in church attendance in North America. Approximately eighty to eighty-five percent of churches are either plateaued or in decline. Churches that at one time had fully-funded pastors must now seek pastors who are willing to be bivocational. Pastor Search Committees frequently contact my office for information on how to work with bivocational pastors. One of the issues is expectations which will be addressed in a later chapter.

Many More Churches Needed in North America

The number of Southern Baptist churches per population is in steady decline. To reverse this trend, Dr. Kevin Ezell, President of the North American Mission Board of the SBC, challenged the SBC Convention messengers meeting in New Orleans in June 2012, to increase the total number of SBC churches in North America by 5,000 in the next 10 years. He stated that since we are losing 810 churches each year, we must start 13,500 churches to reach the goal—or a total increase of 5,000 by 2022.[2] How can this be accomplished? The answer is to challenge more young men to be open to God's call to follow Jesus in becoming fishers of men. Churches are a natural product of people coming to Christ in a local community.

God is calling men with other careers to begin preaching and teaching His Word. These men will need ministerial training but will not be leaving their current vocation. If God is calling them, we must be willing to validate their call and work to equip them to take pastoral leadership as opportunities arise. Doctors, lawyers, accountants, school teachers and a host of other professionals are entering the ministry in surprising numbers. God has a plan. We must be wise enough to recognize it, careful not to hinder it, and mature enough to join Him in making it happen.

2 Ibid

Chapter 4

Advantages & Disadvantages of Bivocational Ministry

The information in this chapter is intended to help a church understand some of the dynamics of calling a bivocational pastor. It will also give insight into moving from bivocational to fully-funded and fully-funded to bivocational. Below is a list of reasons why a church would call a bivocational pastor:

- **Limited finances.** If the church income is not sufficient to pay the pastor an adequate salary, calling a bivocational pastor can be the answer. Finances can be limited by the size of the membership, changes in the community, building debt, high maintenance costs and limited space for growth. A church is not a fully-funded church if the pastor is asked to live on an inadequate salary or his wife has to work outside the home so that he can pastor the church.

- **The field is small.** Many churches are located in sparsely populated communities. When the church field is small and the prospects for church growth are few, a bivocational pastor would be a perfect option. This situation would be an excellent opportunity for the pastor to have greater influence in the community if he were a school teacher, guidance counselor or holds a community service position.

- **The church selects a pastor who feels called to a dual role.** This pastor has a call to pastor and a call in another vocation. Some feel God would have them work at a second vocation to free more church funds for ministry and missions. Sometimes in the selection process some churches decide on a pastor who wants to remain bivocational even though the church can afford to fully-fund his position. This most often proves to be a win—win for both church and pastor.

Items to Consider When Calling a Bivocational Pastor

Both the church and pastor must have a positive attitude toward bivocational status. The church must not feel that it is getting a second class pastor and the pastor must be committed to giving his best to the church.

Both the church and pastor must understand the role each is to play. One of the most frequent sources of conflict between a bivo pastor and the church he serves is unmet expectations. In the following chapter, expectations will be discussed in detail.

Numerous leadership roles must be assumed by the church membership. Too often a fully-funded pastor is expected to provide leadership in almost every area of church life. That is not a healthy model and it is impossible for a bivo pastor. The model presented in Ephesians 4:11-12 makes the pastor the equipper so that the membership does the work of ministry.

> *"And he gave some, apostles; and some, prophets; and some evangelists; and some, pastors and teachers; for the perfecting of the saints, for the work of the ministry, for the edifying of the body of Christ"* (Ephesians 4:11-12).

The bivocational pastor must be one who is not afraid of hard work, who manages his time well and who does not feel the need to control everything in the church. I have often said that a bivo pastor can be many things but he cannot be lazy. Time management is critical and will be discussed in a later chapter.

The Advantages of Bivocational Status

- ■ The financial base of both church and pastor is usually stronger. When staff expenses are kept to around thirty-five or forty percent of the total church budget, much more money will be available for ministry, outreach and missions. The pastor's family can live with less financial strain when there are two incomes.

- The bivocational pastor often experiences greater freedom to lead because non-supportive leadership can not threaten his total livelihood.

- More laity, of necessity, becomes involved in the ministry of the church.

- The bivocational pastor is usually more in touch with the real world.

- The bivocational pastor has more opportunities for personal witnessing.

- Because of time constraints it is less likely that the bivocational pastor will succumb to the temptation to become lazy.

- The bivocational pastor does not have the time to become involved in convention controversy.

- The church is more apt to allow their bivocational pastor to be real.

- Often, the bivocational pastor's family has a more flexible social life.

- Bivocational pastors are more often able to plan and work toward reasonable goals.

- Bivocational pastors usually have adequate health insurance provided by their other employer.

The Advantages of Vocational or Fully-Funded Status

- The fully-funded pastor has more time for sermon preparation, visitation, counseling and local ministry.

- The fully-funded pastor is able to focus entirely on the ministry of the church.

- The fully-funded pastor has more opportunities to attend pastors' conferences, conventions, retreats, conferences, fellowship meetings, training events and a host of other opportunities.

- The fully-funded pastor can respond more quickly to a crisis in the church or community.

- The fully-funded pastor can be available for more one-on-one discipling and mentoring.

- The fully-funded pastor can establish a more realistic routine for meals and family activities.

- The full-funded pastor is more likely to be involved in the various activities of children and grandchildren.

Things to be Considered When Moving from Bivocational to Fully-Funded Status

There is much more involved when moving from bivocational to fully-funded status than simply increasing the pastor's salary a few hundred or thousand dollars. The goal should be to make it possible for the pastor to live on the same level as the average church member. Attention should be given to housing, insurance, disability, conference and convention expenses and retirement.

Many churches do their pastor a disservice by giving him a pay "package" and allowing him to decide how it is to be broken down. For one thing, the church thinks they are paying their pastor more than they really are if they do not see how much goes for necessary expenses before anything is left for actual salary. Also, if the salary is less than sufficient the pastor will probably not get adequate insurance and ignore his retirement funding. A church should automatically cover health insurance, basic life insurance, retirement funding and ministerial expenses before discussing salary and housing for their pastor.

Just because a pastor moves from bivocational to give full attention to the church does not mean he automatically becomes superman. He cannot visit all the sick, homebound and prospects, keep up the church facilities and grounds, lead every program, run the church office and be fully prepared to preach God's Word two or even three times a week. An agreement should be reached about personal time. It is wise to take some time off each week because the weekend is normally very busy and demanding.

Should a Church Move from Fully-Funded to Bivocational?

When a church is in a declining situation and unable to maintain the facilities and fully fund a pastor, it should not consider calling a bivocational pastor as a step backward. Actually the church has already taken a step backward. Calling a bivocational pastor is a step forward. More and more pastors are sensing a call to serve bivocationally. Since the biblical model of bivocational ministry is presented through the Apostle Paul, no pastor or church should feel inadequate because of bivocational leadership.

The advantages of being bivocational as presented earlier should be given closer examination. Often a Director of Missions or convention staff person can provide counsel and insight in making the transition in this direction. If a church is to be successful in calling a bivocational pastor which provides the leadership it needs, it must first reach agreements regarding "Items to Consider" as stated earlier, and "Expectations" as discussed in the next chapter. Calling a bivocational pastor can bring relief, satisfaction and a new sense of direction to a church which has struggled for years to maintain a fully-funded status for their pastor.

Chapter 5

Dealing with Expectations

One of the primary sources of conflict and disappointment in any relationship is unmet expectations. To minimize this problem the parties must communicate, often and fully, concerning roles, feelings and desires. It is estimated that seventy-five percent of marriage conflicts could be resolved through better communication.

It has frequently been stated that we usually are down on things we are not up on. This means that we would have a different opinion if we had all the facts. This is expressed in the old Indian proverb: "Do not criticize another until you have walked in his moccasins for a week." Disappointment with another due to unmet expectations does not prove a flaw in the person or actions of another individual. For example, Mary and Martha were disappointed with Jesus because He had not come when they first sent for Him. They did not understand that Jesus planned to raise Lazarus from the dead, not just the sick bed.

The two men on the road to Emmaus were disappointed that Jesus had died on a cross instead of delivering Israel from the Romans. Jesus explained to them that God's plan for Israel included more than an earthly kingdom. He was going to build an eternal kingdom that included redeemed people from all nations. He had to die to make that possible. As we look back over our lives, all of us can be thankful for the prayers God did not answer.

In order for a bivocational pastor and the church he serves to have a productive and lengthy relationship, there needs to be a clear understanding of what to expect by both parties. Expectations between a bivo pastor and his church can be called a two-way street. They each need to know what they can expect from one another.

What a Church Should Expect from a Bivocational Pastor

- **The church should expect their pastor to be a strong man of character.** This should be a given among all ministers. Experience has taught that nothing should be taken for granted anymore. Too many pastors have run off with the church's money or its secretary. Every church should do a background check on each staff member before hiring. There should never be a serious question to the moral purity of a man of God.

- **The church should expect honesty, trustworthiness, and a strong work ethic.** Dr. Adrian Rogers once said that the most important trait in a pastor should be integrity. If a pastor cuts corners on the truth or fails to keep confidence with the membership and others he will lose his credibility and thus his ability to be a positive influence. He must not be afraid of hard work. A reputation of laziness is difficult to live down.

■ **A church should expect their pastor to believe and preach the Word of God.** The church should be clear that their prospective pastor realizes that his authority comes from the Word and not what he thinks or feels. The Word of God is the only acceptable food for the flock of God. The difference between a man of God and a false prophet is his commitment to God's written Word.

■ **A church should expect their pastor to be a man of prayer and faith.** No pastor can effectively lead without continual input from his Commander in Chief. There can be no direction or spiritual power without prayer. He must believe God himself before he can convince others to trust Him.

■ **A church should expect their pastor to set a good example by loving and leading his own family.** The world is in desperate need of models demonstrating how to live successfully as a family. The church is not exempt from divorce and family conflict. The Bible is very specific concerning the need for pastors to love and lead their families. Possibly the greatest message a pastor will ever preach is the one lived through his wife, children and grandchildren.

■ **A church should expect their pastor to love them.** The Bible is very clear *"Christ also loved the church and gave himself for it"* (Ephesians 5:25). If a pastor is to be an obedient under-shepherd for the Good Shepherd, he must love the church he pastors. People will be willing to trust and follow a pastor who loves them. They will also be more willing to give him slack regarding his short-comings if they know he operates out of love for them.

■ **A church should expect their pastor to have a fresh word from God each time he stands to speak.** The most important role of a pastor is to feed the flock God has put in his trust. There are many good things a pastor can do but if he does not have a fresh word from God when he stands to preach, he has failed in his primary calling. Priorities must be established so that he will be able to share a fresh message from God when he stands before them.

■ **A church should expect their pastor to provide them with vision and leadership.** God has always called and worked through leaders to accomplish His purpose through His people. Sheep must have a shepherd. The shepherd must stay before God until he finds the direction he is to lead the flock. The children of Israel are not the only people of God who have done a lot of wandering around in circles.

■ **A church should expect their pastor to protect them from error and false prophets.** The Apostle Paul and other leaders of the early church were continually warning believers of the doctrinal error and deception of false prophets. There have always been wolves in sheep's clothing. The Bible teaches that doctrinal error and false prophets will be on the increase during the last days. Each pastor must realize that he will give an account to God for each church he pastors (Hebrews 13:17).

- **Each church with a bivo pastor should have a general agreement on the amount of time he will spend on study, ministry and church administration.** For the bivo pastor most study and sermon preparation will probably be done at home. He should announce if he can manage some time at the church office each week so the people will know when he can best be reached. The total amount of time a bivocational pastor can give to his pastoral duties will usually average twenty hours per week. It could go as high as thirty depending on his other vocation.

- **A church with a bivocational pastor should expect him to have a key leader in place to respond quickly to a church or community crisis.** Most bivocational pastors do not have the flexibility to drop everything and respond to every crisis that arises. Some churches rotate their deacons and publish the schedule along with telephone numbers in the weekly bulletin. The church should establish a plan for contacting everyone, including the pastor, in order to begin praying and ministering in the event of a need.

- **A church that is led by a bivocational pastor should expect him to train lay leaders to assume ministry** responsibilities. Every church needs members who have been trained to lead various ministries of the church. This is especially true of a church with a bivocational pastor. The scriptures are clear that a basic role of the pastor is to train members to do the work of the ministry (Ephesians 4:1-16). Often members whose pastor is bivocational are more ready to step forward because they realize the pastor cannot do everything.

What a Bivocational Pastor Should Expect from the Church

■ **The pastor should expect the church to pray for him.** One of the most crucial needs of a spiritual leader is for those he leads to pray for him. No pastor has ever had more prayer than he could use. It is often true that we seldom pray for those we criticize and we seldom criticize those for whom we pray. The task of pastoring a church is overwhelming without the assurance of divine assistance.

■ **The pastor should expect the church to respect the position he holds.** Respect for those in ministry is at an all time low in this country. God has always demanded that His chosen leaders be treated with dignity and respect. A man of God should be respected because of the One he represents.

■ **The pastor should expect his church to love him and his family.** A pastor is a servant by nature of his calling. He has a God-given desire to serve and meet the needs of others. A church should love the man who is giving himself to them on a daily basis. His family needs to be loved and appreciated without unrealistic expectations. It is so difficult to be a pastor's wife and family. Make their lives easier by assuring them of your love and support.

■ **The pastor should expect the church to protect his good name.** The reputation of a pastor is pivotal to the effectiveness of his ministry. The Bible gives specific guidelines about listening to gossip about a pastor *"Against an elder receive not an accusation, but before two or three witnesses. Them that sin rebuke before all, that others also may fear."* (I Timothy 5:19-20). Praying for your pastor is much more productive than criticizing him. Demand proof before allowing attacks on the character of a pastor.

■ **A pastor should expect his church to follow his leadership.** A person is not a leader unless someone is following. A man that God places as the leader of a specific flock should rightly expect the flock to follow his leadership. The Bible is full of examples of stiff-necked people who refused to follow the leader God gave them. A person should be very careful to have definite Biblical grounds before refusing to follow the leader God gave him.

■ **A pastor should expect that his church understand and accept his bivocational status with its advantages and disadvantages.** God has a specific man prepared to lead a specific church for a specific time. Just any man will not do. A church needs to find God's man for them. Some of those men will be bivocational. A church can get into a lot of trouble by mistreating the man God sent. It is a tragedy that often a church does not appreciate their pastor until he is gone. A church should do its best to help the pastor make the church the best it can be.

■ **A bivocational pastor should expect the church to be thankful he is willing to work another job so they can have a pastor.** Most church members fail to appreciate just how demanding it is to serve as a bivocational pastor. He is busy working or ministering while they are watching television or enjoying a family outing. Some bivocational pastors prepare their messages after midnight in order to allow a little time with family.

■ **A bivocational pastor should expect his church membership to understand that his primary responsibility is to provide for the needs of his family to the best of his ability.** A good pastor cannot be paid too much. The Bible says that a faithful pastor is worthy of double honor or double income, *"Let the elders that rule well be counted worthy of double honor, especially they who labour in the word and doctrine."* (I Timothy 5:17). Someone jokingly told of a church member who prayed, *"Lord, bless our poor, humble preacher. You keep him humble and we will keep him poor."* The pay should be as generous as the church can afford. The compensation package should include salary, housing, insurance, auto expenses, professional expenses and retirement. I have included as an Appendix an information piece prepared by my good friend, Richard Skidmore, who serves the Tennessee Baptist Convention as Financial Support Specialist. This is designed to help a church do a better job of planning the compensation for their pastor. You might find this information helpful.

■ **A bivocational pastor should expect the church membership to faithfully support the church with their attendance, service and giving.** How would you like to lead a church full of folks who were just like you? Acts 2:1 is the dream of every pastor. He would love to see all the church gathered together in one accord. If every member tithed all churches would have the means to do everything God wants them to do.

■ **The bivocational pastor needs to know that the church understands he cannot be available for every surgery, sickness or crisis.** The expectations expressed by many church members concerning what they believe their bivocational pastor should do are not very realistic. The average church places more demands on the pastor than the Bible. There are many times when a phone call and prayer over the phone should be sufficient. It is almost as if some church members play a game with their pastor. If they can go to the hospital and get out before He finds out and visits, they win! How refreshing for a member to actually tell their pastor ahead of time about hospital visits or tests and let him know a visit is not necessary but prayers are welcome.

■ **The pastor expects the church to understand that he will not neglect his family while serving the church.** It is sad to see what being in the ministry has done to many pastor's children and often their wives. God never intended for the greatest call on a man's life to become the greatest curse on his family. The church should encourage and applaud their pastor when he gives priority to his wife and children.

■ **The pastor expects the church to accept lay leadership when he is not available.** Often church members gripe and complain when a deacon or other church leader makes hospital or home visits. Those authorized by the pastor to visit or lead in his place should be received with appreciation for their efforts and respect for the pastor's efforts to delegate responsibilities and train lay leaders.

Without a doubt there are many things that could be added to this chapter. Nevertheless, these items provide a realistic beginning. Regardless of how much is discussed initially other concerns will arise as time progresses. A plan should be in place to discuss these and resolve them. Both need to have the freedom to communicate concerns without anyone feeling threatened, defensive or judgmental. A pastor advisory team, church leadership team, or the deacon body could be utilized to deal with these issues.

Chapter 6

Bivocational Pastors Do More Than Preach

There is a big difference between being the preacher at a church and the pastor of a church. Every church can benefit from having a great preacher occasionally. However, every church needs a pastor or shepherd who will provide leadership at all times. Their pastor may or may not be a great preacher, but if he loves them, leads them and feeds them, they are blessed indeed. To be absolutely honest, some bivo preachers have a preaching station not a pastorate. They serve the church more as a chaplain than a pastor. They show up at the church to preach at each service but do nothing else to shepherd the church.

It's a sad truth, but many of the church folks like it that way. They attend church usually on Sunday morning, but do not want to be bothered during the rest of the week. The Biblical model for church is for the pastor to shepherd the flock. In the Old Testament, God presented Himself as Shepherd for His flock, Israel.

> *"Behold, the Lord God will come with strong hand, and His arm shall rule for him: behold, His reward is with Him, and His work before Him. He shall feed His flock like a shepherd: he will gather the lambs with His arms, and carry them in His bosom, and shall gently lead those that are with young"* (Isaiah 48:10-11).

In the New Testament Jesus Christ is called *"the good Shepherd"* (John 10:11), *"the great Shepherd"* (Hebrews 13:20) and *"the chief Shepherd"* (I Peter 5:4). Peter challenges elders, whom most Bible students believe are pastors, to do their work as a faithful shepherd.

> *"The elders which are among you I exhort, who am also an elder, and a witness of the sufferings of Christ, and also a partaker of the glory that shall be revealed. Feed the flock of God which is among you, taking the oversight thereof, not by constraint, but willingly; not for filthy lucre, but of a ready mine; neither as being lords over God's heritage, but examples to the flock. And when the chief Shepherd shall appear, ye shall receive a crown of glory that fadeth not away"* (I Peter 5:1-4).

Being the shepherd of a flock of God's sheep is an awesome responsibility. It has the potential to bring great blessing but it can also bring tremendous heartache. Jesus Christ is the Chief Shepherd and all pastors are to follow His example and serve under His supervision. I feel that we should examine some of the jobs assigned to the shepherd of God's flock.

Feed the Flock

I am fully convinced that the primary responsibility of a pastor is to feed the flock God has entrusted to him. The Bible is a big book. The pastor must find the right word from God for his people and share it in such a way that they can digest the message. It is the responsibility of the sheep to come to be fed. If they are not fed regularly, they become spiritually weak. This does not mean that members should not be feeding themselves daily. But God gives a special word in the corporate worship time. A good pastor will help his people develop a hunger for the meat of the Word.

Lead the Flock

A shepherd is not a shepherd unless he is leading the flock. If no one is following him, he is not a leader. He is just taking a walk. When a flock does not have a leader, they will stray. It should be a constant prayer of a pastor that God would show him how to lead and where to lead the flock. The church should pray daily that God would direct their leader. Leading the flock includes receiving and sharing a vision for the future. A member of the flock should have a very good reason to resist or criticize the leading of their shepherd. Paul gives some strong advice in I Timothy 5:17-20 about how we are to handle criticism of a pastor.

Oversee the Flock

The pastor is the overseer of the church whether he wants to be or not. The writer of Hebrews uses the term "rule" (Hebrews 13:7, 17). Pastors are not to be dictators but gentle shepherds. They will give an account to God for how they led the flock. This oversight includes providing direction and requiring account-ability from staff members or lay leaders. Many churches suffer from what has been jokingly referred to as "staff infection." All staff members must be supportive of the pastor and respectful of the authority of his position.

Carry the Little Lambs

The pastor is to carry the little lambs. This is what God said in Isaiah that He did to the nation of Israel. Newborn Christians need a lot of attention. They must be nurtured and helped to grow. Mature Christians should not expect the pastor to spend nearly as much time with them as he does with new converts. The first six months after conversion are perhaps the most critical in a Christian's development. Jesus made a very strong statement when He said that it be better for a man to be at the bottom of the lake than to offend one of these little ones that believe in Him (Matthew 18:6). These little ones require gentle care and the message conveyed here is that the shepherd knows the needs of each one and how to lead them.

Restore the Lost Sheep

Jesus described the heart of a good shepherd in John 15, when He said that a good shepherd will go looking for the one lost sheep even though ninety-nine are safely in the fold. Sheep are not very smart animals.

They have a tendency to stray from the fold but do not have the sense of direction to get back home. The shepherd must go looking for them. God was very disappointed in the prophets of the Old Testament who were poor shepherds.

> *"Woe is unto the pastors that destroy and scatter the sheep of my pasture, saith the Lord. Therefore thus saith the Lord God of Israel against the pastors that feed my people; ye have scattered my flock and driven them away, and have not visited them; behold I will visit upon you the evil of your doings, saith the Lord. And I will gather the remnant of my flock out of all countries whether I have driven them and will bring them again to their folds; and they shall be fruitful and increase and I will set up shepherds over them which shall feed them; and they shall fear no more, nor be dismayed, neither shall they be lacking, saith the Lord."* Jeremiah 23:1-4

The shepherd's staff was used to correct wayward sheep. Pastors should do all they can to restore wayward sheep even if they must be brutally frank. When they are restored there should be a joyful celebration.

Fight Off the Wolves

Sheep do not have the ability to defend themselves. Sheep must have the shepherd's protection. Wolves are always around waiting for an opportunity to devour the sheep. The true shepherd will chase away the wolves that are stalking his sheep (John 10:11-12). Those who are doing it for money will flee. Our Shepherd laid down His life for the sheep. Wolves will certainly come when the shepherd is not around (Acts 20:28-31). Wolves often come dressed like sheep but you can identify them by their fruit (Matthew 7:15-20). The sheep are more easily deceived than the shepherd because he knows how to watch for them.

Keep the Sheep Together Until the Chief Shepherd Appears

God has many sheepfolds (John 10:11). The shepherd's job is not finished until his flock gets together in heaven with the other flocks. When pastors get to heaven, the Chief Shepherd will relieve them of their responsibilities.

The responsibilities just described prove that a pastor is more than a preacher. All preachers love to preach, but many are not as excited or committed to the other roles of a pastor. A bivocational pastor must keep this in mind as he accepts the challenge to be the shepherd of a flock of God's sheep.

Chapter 7

Being a Life-Long Student

Have you ever had someone ask you where you received your education. They usually want to know where you went to seminary. I am often tempted to begin with the very first school I attended, Susie P. Trigg Elementary, and recite the long list of schools, colleges, seminary, online courses, Bible studies, and seminars I have been a part of for the past fifty years. I still consider myself an ignorant and unlearned man, but I have been with Jesus. The truth is—we should never stop learning. As men of God we should commit to being life-long students. It has been stated that a call to preach is a call to prepare. Paul made this very clear when he wrote to the young preacher Timothy. *"Study to show thyself* *approved unto God, a workman that needeth not to be ashamed, rightly dividing the Word of Truth"* (II Timothy 2:15). Those who fail to adequately prepare limit their ability to be used!

Do Not Justify Poor Study Habits

Some had adamantly stated that they do not need to study. God just gives them what to say when they stand up to preach. They may be referring to something Jesus said but are taking it out of context. In Luke 12:11, 12 Jesus said, *"and when they bring you unto magistrates, and powers, take ye no thought how or what thing ye shall answer or what ye shall say: For the Holy Ghost shall teach you in the same hour what ye ought to say."* Jesus was not talking about preaching but about making a defense for yourself when being persecuted for your witness for Christ. Those who do not study and prepare usually end up saying the same thing over and over no matter what their starting text.

Get As Much Formal Education As You Can

Looking back over my many years of ministry, I can advise you to get as much training as you can as early as possible. The longer you put it off, the more difficult it will be. I speak from experience when I say your formal education is much easier to get before you have the responsibility and expense of a family. There are many avenues of training. The traditional is college and then seminary. For economy and convenience some choose correspondence studies or seminary extension. Today online training is becoming more and more popular because of the accessibility. Students can study from home at their own pace and during hours that agree with their schedule. Full degree programs are available without ever leaving home. The cafeteria approach to education is great and if that works for you, go for it. There are many educational tools available. Choose the ones that are right for you and become a life- long student.

One of the basic purposes of formal education is to teach you how to study. A good student will have an eternal quest for knowledge. Always keep you mind sharp. No one ever fully masters the Word of God. It is foolish for a preacher to think he has complete understanding of a particular verse or set of verses because he has preached a sermon or series of sermons from that text. Take advantage of seminars, conferences, and short-term training events. Your church deserves to hear fresh material.

Study books are the tools of a minister. You need to get good ones and learn how to use them. Balance your study between modern and time-tested scholars. Word study helps are of great benefit. I have been surprised at the meager library of many pastors. Did you hear the joke about a preacher who lost his whole library in a fire? His whole library was destroyed—all three books. But the bad thing was that he had not yet colored in one of them!

Many study helps are available online and many Bible study programs can be purchased making owning hard copies not as important or necessary as it once was. Make regular trips to the bookstore to see what new materials have come out. Just like a carpenter needs to keep up with the new tools available, the preacher needs to take advantage of fresh study materials. I am usually studying four or five books at once. A great Bible teacher once told me that if he got just one good thought or illustration from a book, it was worth the price he paid for it.

Find a Mentor

Jesus Christ was the most effective teacher to walk the face of this earth. He took twelve men and turned the world upside down. He did not have a syllabus for training His disciples or a formal school through which they were taught. Here is what the scriptures say: *"And He goeth up into a mountain, and called unto him whom he would; and they came unto him. And he ordained twelve that they should be with him, and that he might send them forth to preach"* (Mark 3:13, 14). The key training tool was to be with Him and watch how He did things. This is called mentoring. Every young preacher needs a mentor. The Apostle Paul is a great example in his mentoring of Timothy. We learn from others that God is using even as we grow older. Mentoring is mutually beneficial. Younger men of God can teach those of us who are older a lot about passion, enthusiasm, and vision.

One of the brightest minds that God ever used to share His Word was the Apostle Paul. It appears that he remained a student throughout his life. He closed his second letter to Timothy by requesting that Timothy bring his cloak, his books and especially his parchments (II Timothy 4:3).

Getting into a rut and operating from habit or routine is sometimes a tendency for those who have been in the ministry for a long time. Living in a rut is not an exciting way to live life as a servant of God. Remaining a life-long student will insure an element of freshness and anticipation of greater effectiveness in the days ahead.

Chapter 8

The Need for Balance

There is no higher purpose than to invest one's life in the ministry of the Gospel. The Prophet Isaiah said that all who share the Gospel have beautiful feet (Isaiah 5:2-7). These feet enable them to carry the Gospel message. The life of a messenger today involves much more than the proclamation of the Gospel. The minister feels pressure from many areas of his life and work. The bivocational pastor finds himself trying to juggle church, family and work. He cannot give all the time he feels he should to any one area. He tries to work harder and faster, but feels himself getting further and further behind. He may wake up one morning and realize that his life is out of balance. Stress levels have begun to rise and the joy of ministry is replaced with trying to get through the day.

Many factors contribute to the feeling of imbalance. I want to focus on the four major ones. The first is **financial pressure**. Financial pressure can slowly eat away at a minister's sense of well-being. Many ministers are expected to live on less than adequate compensation. As discussed earlier, the church should clearly understand the actual amount of salary the pastor is left with to support his family after covering expenses related to being a minister. Along with the other factors mentioned, a church should be aware that a pastor pays twice the percentage of Social Security tax than the average person because he is considered self employed..

Another contributing factor to financial pressure is the accumulation of debt. Today credit is so easy to get that it can be very tempting to use it as a way out of financial pressure or to live above your means. However, acquiring debt irresponsibly is destructive. Unpaid debt will affect every area of your life. Develop a financial plan and learn to live within your means. One option to help alleviate some financial pressure for the bivocational pastor is to find a higher paying job. Most of all, don't blame God for your poor financial choices.

The family is the second area where the bivocational pastor needs balance. There are so many things that compete for the bivocational pastor's time. In attempting to juggle family, work and church he often makes the critical mistake of short changing his family for the sake of trying to be an effective minister to the church and community. The wife will be the first to vocalize her feelings and the pastor would be wise to take heed. Stress in marriage will take a toll on the entire family and is a constant drain on emotional energy.

Many pastors are too busy to spend quality time with their children. The children develop resentment and a rebellious attitude toward their father and the church. I still counsel with a preacher's son that I grew up with who has hated his dad since he was a child because his dad never had time for him. It's difficult enough for a preacher's children even when their father is there for them. When family members resent the ministry you have a hard time feeling good about yourself or your ministry. Being absent from many, if not most, family activities will produce discord. It is difficult to minister to other families when your own family is not what it should be.

The third area a pastor needs to balance is his **fear of the opinions of people**. A pastor has the unenviable task of having to correct and challenge the people who pay his salary. Worry about what they will say or do sometimes keeps him from doing his best. I discovered this truth at the young age of twenty-seven. I went to the doctor and discovered I had developed an ulcer. My doctor told me, "The problem is not what you've been eating but what's been eating you." Pleasing God should always take precedence over pleasing others. I have discovered that trying to please others is a no-win situation. We must focus on doing what is right and let the chips fall where they will. You cannot minister with confidence when you have a fear of people. Fear produces torment. You can never enjoy your ministry if you are controlled by a fear of people.

The fourth area that tends to get out of balance is the area of **our commitments**. Ministers are givers by nature. We want to help and make a difference. When asked to do something the typical pastor will respond with, "I will do what I can," or "I will make it work somehow." The last thing he wants to do is say "no." This often leads to over commitment. When we allow ourselves to become overcommitted, we find ourselves doing less than our best in many areas. Ministers must learn to delegate when possible or say "no" without guilt when necessary.

Keys to Achieving Balance

There is no one adjustment which can produce balance and there is no one time fix. Achieving balance in your life as a minister is something that requires constant determination and vigilance. We are going to look at twelve keys that I believe will be of help, but this is by no means an exhaustive list.

- **Put God first in your life.** Nothing is more important than your own walk with God. There must be daily Bible study and prayer to feed your own soul before thinking about preaching to others. Guard against thinking about a sermon while having personal devotions. Sermons will certainly come out of your personal time with God but sermon preparation should be kept separate from your quiet time. This is the reason why it is so easy to backslide in seminary or Bible College. Students think that studying courses on the Bible make personal devotions unnecessary.

- **Establish priorities.** First in the order of your basic priorities should be your personal relationship with God. Everything else flows from our personal relationship with God. After your time with God is prioritized, your list should come in this order: your spouse, your children, your church and your work. Some bivocational pastors make the mistake of believing that the church comes before their wife and children. Nothing could be farther from the mind of God. If you lose your church you still have your family. But if you lose your family you will probably not still have your church. A pastor would be wise to hear these words from the Song of Solomon; *"they made me keeper of the vineyards; but mine own vineyard have I not kept"* (Song of Solomon 1:6b). We as pastors must realize that we cannot do everything that is expected of us. However, we can focus on what is most important.

- **Link your calling to your calendar.** Block out specific periods of time for your primary work. The primary work of a pastor is to feed the sheep (I Peter 5:1-4). Do an evaluation at the end of each day to see how you used your time. Another suggestion that I have used successfully is to take time out for a planning retreat. Take your wife with you. She is a vital part of your scheduling and planning, plus you will have some time together. A planning retreat, perhaps, twice a year will help you stay focused and energized.

- **Have a clear purpose and direction for your life.** Make sure you are where you feel you should be, doing what you feel you should be doing. Be yourself. Realize that God made you to be the person He wanted you to be. Learn to be comfortable with yourself and your life. Don't compare yourself with others or try to imitate others. Jesus is our greatest example of always being controlled by what we are here to do. Set goals for things you want to accomplish and work toward those goals.

■ **Be proactive rather than reactive.** Plan your life and live out your plan. My wife and I are risk takers. We have never been satisfied with the status quo. We like to live in the realm of possibilities. We believe that nothing is impossible when we are following God's lead. Learn to be in control of your life instead of allowing others to call the shots. Invest your time in doing what you feel God would have you do instead of following the dictates of others.

■ **Maintain a clear conscience.** Determine to live an open, honest and transparent life. Do not allow yourself to be in a position where you are controlled by the fear that something you have done will be discovered. Know in your heart that you have done your best to do the right thing in all circumstances. Integrity is a vital quality in the life of a man of God.

■ **Find an accountability partner.** Find someone with whom you can be totally honest and completely confidential. Interact with your accountability partner often so he knows what is going on in your life. Ask him to check up on you and hold you accountable. I have had several accountability partners in my life and I can tell you I value their love and friendship, but more than that, I value their honesty and willingness to hold me accountable.

■ **Have a family council.** Meet with your family at least once a week to make sure things are going as they should. Seek honest input and refuse to become defensive. Listen to your wife. She is the one who has her ear to the ground when it comes to family and church happenings. Value the contribution and council of your family. Show your children that what they feel and say counts.

■ **Find the secret of contentment.** Contentment is not based on our circumstances. Paul wrote from prison that he had learned the secret of being content in any and all circumstances (Philippians 4:11-13). Sometimes we might feel that our circumstances are a prison. Changing our circumstances is not the answer to our discontentment. God is the God of our circumstances and He can work in spite of them to accomplish His will through us. We must learn to become Christ-sufficient and not self-sufficient.

■ **Realize you are not superman.** I have heard folks say "I had rather burn out than rust out." A better alternative to either of these options is to "finish out" or "finish well." People will allow you to do as much as you are willing to do and applaud you for it. A better goal is quality not quantity. We need to strive for significance not super-achievement. We are in for the long haul. We need to set our pace and finish well.

■ **Make regular deposits into your emotional bank.** Ministry depletes your emotional bank. If you keep making withdrawals without making a deposit, you will have an overdraft. Our son, Stephen, was killed in an automobile accident on a Tuesday. His funeral was on Thursday, and I was back in the pulpit on Sunday, while my wife was back in her class the next Sunday. We had never lost a child. All we knew to do was to keep on keeping on. We should have taken time off to grieve—to get our souls back in our bodies. We were empty. We kept going through the motions, but we had nothing to give. Whether you need to grieve; take time away with your family; get more rest and relaxation or just have some fun replenish your emotional bank regularly.

- **Do what you do as unto the Lord.** Doing whatever you do unto the Lord elevates the importance of your efforts (Colossians 3:23-24). Let Him be your judge and refuse to settle for lower court opinions. Do what you do with all your heart. The real payday will be at the Judgment Seat of Christ. Only then will you receive your full reward.

Keeping your life in balance is not easy for a minister. We must be like the distance runner who keeps his eyes on the finish line. We should seek to be able to say like the Apostle Paul, "*I have finished my course*" (II Timothy 4:6-7).

Chapter 9

Taking Control of Your Time

The most amazing example of someone being in complete control of His time is Jesus Christ. On one occasion He told His disciples, *"My time has not yet come"* (John 7:6). At another place He said, *"I must work the works of him who sent me, while it is day; the night cometh, when no man can work"* (John 9:4). At the close of His earthly ministry, He said, *"The hour is come that the Son of man should be glorified"* (John 12:23).

Our Lord never was in a hurry. He always had time to help those He met and He never stressed over His busy schedule. The things we enjoy that are supposed to make life easier were non-existent in His day, such as automobiles, telephones, computers, internet, running water, electricity and fast food. If a bivocational pastor is to survive the many demands he faces daily he must learn to take control of his time.

The Number One Issue with Bivo Pastors

I came to work for the Tennessee Baptist Convention in 1992, but in 1995 I began the new assignment of working to encourage, resource and train bivocational pastors in Tennessee. I began by conducting several regional listening sessions and "think tanks" with bivocational pastors. The number one issue in each of those sessions was time management. Everyone wanted help in learning how to make better use of his time.

At the time, I was working full-time for the Convention and serving as interim pastor of a church in McMinnville, Tennessee. The church had just gone through some difficulties and they wanted me to become their pastor. It was the policy of the Convention to allow staff to do interims for a defined period of time. The convention was also looking for someone to fill a new position as Bivocational Ministries Specialist.

My wife, Diane, who has always been my best advisor, told me that I should ask the Convention to allow me to transfer to this new position then I could become bivocational pastor of the church. After several weeks of deliberation it was agreed that I would work a thirty hour week for the Convention. This allowed me to become bivocational pastor at the church. I was supposed to be in my office at the Convention at least one day a week and spend the remainder of the thirty hours traveling and holding training events. The church was fine with my role as bivocational pastor, but this is how it turned out. Staff at the convention building thought I only worked one day a week. The church folks said I was always out of town and my wife said I was never home. Welcome to the life of the bivocational pastor!

Misconceptions about Time

People indicate misconceptions about time when they discuss the challenges they have before them. Have you ever heard some say, "Why don't you ask him to do that for you? He has more time than I do." I recently did an extensive study on time and came up with a startling discovery. We all have twenty-four hours in each day! We all have the same amount of time. The issue is usually the busyness of one compared to the inactivity of another.

We also hear people talk about doing things a certain way "to save time." Time cannot be saved today to use tomorrow. All of the time in this day will be used before we begin tomorrow. What we really mean when we talk about "saving time" is accomplishing a task quicker and more efficiently so that we can perform more tasks.

We occasionally hear someone say they have been "killing time." Time cannot be killed. Regardless of what we do or do not do, time marches on. We may use our time constructively, destructively or in trivial pursuit, but it is used up when the day is over. As a bivocational pastor, I quickly learned to make wise use of my time and guard against procrastination.

Using Your Time Wisely

What the bivocational pastor wants to know is how to make the best use of his time. We all could benefit by praying the prayer Moses prayed is Psalms 90:12, *"So teach us to number our days, that we may apply our hearts to wisdom."* There are so many things that compete for our time each day. We all want to end our day with the feeling we made the wisest use of our time.

A good starting point would be for us to realize that we cannot do everything we would like or that others expect of us. When we understand that, we can develop a plan to make the best use of our time. For most of us that plan means making a "to do" list. Write down and prioritize all the tasks, appointments or things to remember for one day. Systematically work through the list and check off things as they are done. This sounds elementary but it works.

Don't be discouraged if everything on the list doesn't get done. Some tasks take more time than we planned and unforeseen things will come up. Just begin the list for tomorrow with those things that did not get done today.

A good rule to follow when accepting a task or challenge is to realize that we are most effective when we work from our giftedness and motivation. Have you noticed how much you struggle and how hard it is to get started on a project for which you are poorly equipped to handle? This does not mean we should never tackle difficult assignments; just remember to make sure it is a priority before committing to the undertaking.

Learn to Delegate

If anyone needs to be good at delegating it is the bivocational pastor. This is especially true when it comes to the work of the church. Have you noticed how many churches are willing to let the pastor and his wife do everything? Many bivocational pastors and their wives clean the church, cut the grass, prepare the bulletins, unlock and lock the church and lead every ministry of the church in addition to preaching, teaching, administration, visiting the sick, the homebound, new prospects and they respond to every crisis.

Acts 6 gives us an early church account of delegating. The deacons were selected to minister to the needs of the church widows so the apostles could give themselves to prayer and the ministry of the Word. Ephesians 4 teaches us that the pastor is to equip the church members to do the work of ministry. God has placed in every church members who are capable of undertaking some of the work that needs to be done. Pastors are actually cheating the people out of a blessing if they choose to do things other people should be doing.

A key ingredient in delegation is the release of control of everything that takes place in a church. A pastor must be willing to allow a member to make mistakes as he learns to lead. The old phrase "If you want something done right, do it yourself," is not a wise way to lead.

A pastor must learn to present the challenge for folks to volunteer, provide training for those who step forward, hold them accountable, pick them up when they stumble and applaud every step of progress. Believe it or not, there are probably folks in your church who can do certain things better that you!

Learn to Multitask

A bivocational pastor finds himself performing like the man in the circus who sees how many plates he can keep spinning at the same time. Life would be wonderfully simple if we could do just one thing at a time, but, it would probably be very dull. There are times when we need to say with the Apostle Paul, *"This one thing I do…"* (Philippians 3:13).

Some things are so important that we have to forget everything else at the moment and concentrate on the great challenge before us. However, during most of his day, the bivo pastor finds himself trying to do several things at once.

Bivocational pastors have to learn to change mental gears frequently. One pastor I know carries two cell phones. One is his church phone and the other his construction business phone. He said he answers each phone differently.

After almost eighteen years as a bivocational pastor I have learned somewhat to compartmentalize my many areas of responsibility. When I have a pressing assignment I disconnect from unrelated tasks. When that job is finished, I refocus and bring everything else up to speed. I learned to do that out of necessity. I felt like I was drowning and I had to learn to keep my head above water.

A bivocational pastor learns to make every minute count. I always take whatever book I am currently studying with me when I have my car serviced or go to the doctor's office. There's no way to count the number of sermons I have prepared while in my car traveling from one assignment to the next. Years ago my son, Stephen, gave me a hand held recorder for that purpose because he was concerned about me making sermon notes while driving.

Guard Against Time Wasters

The bivocational pastor must be on guard and protect himself against time wasters that creep into his day. Unnecessarily long telephone conversations can be a time waster. Sometimes people with nothing better to do will come into your office and monopolize your day if you let them.

The internet can be a very good thing, but if you are not careful browsing the internet can quickly consume hours of your day. Playing games on your phone, computer or television are not bad things to do with your children, but they are a major source of wasted time for many people. Work time and play time should be given their rightful place in the life of the bivocational pastor. Pastors need to learn how to have a good time, but there is a time for everything.

Ending the Day Well

Have you ever come to the end of a busy day only to look back and wonder what you actually accomplished?

I have.

You probably stressed over the things you did not get done.

I still do sometimes.

It is important to our health and well-being that we learn to end the day well. I have learned that it helps me to go back to the list I made at the start of the day and check off the things that did get done. Then I celebrate everything I was able to accomplish. I find it very positive and satisfying to be able to acknowledge the things I accomplish that day.

Don't beat yourself up over the things you could not do!

Honestly, the list we make at the start of the day is usually unrealistic. However, it does provide a plan of action—and that's a good thing.

Next, make a new list in order of priority for tomorrow!

As you prepare to rest for the night, say to yourself, "I have had a good day. I believe I gave it my best."

Chapter 10

Being Yourself

A number of bivocational pastors struggle with identity crisis. They are unsure about their roles as bivocational pastors, preachers in the workplace, and husbands and fathers who are gone a lot of the time. Some think that because they are not fully-funded they are not as successful as other pastors.

I have observed pastors for fifty years and have concluded that some of the greatest men of God are serving in small congregations in obscure places and have never received public recognition. They just faithfully serve God to the best of their ability. Obviously, God's standard of success is drastically different from ours. When are we ever going to accept the fact that God is keeping the only scorecard that matters?

The true source of our self-worth and significance is not what we have done or the size of the church we serve. Our real identify rests in who God says we are, and what He feels about us. Psalm 139 is one of my "go to" scriptures when I lose sight of who I am. Look at what David said about himself and apply it to you and me today.

> *"For you created my inmost being; you knit me together in my mother's womb. I praise you because I am fearfully and wonderfully made; your works are wonderful, I know that full well. My frame was not hidden from you when I was made in the secret place. When I was woven together in the depths of the earth, your eyes saw my unformed body. All the days ordained for me were written in your book before one of them came to be"* (Psalms 139:13-16 NIV).

God personally put you together in your mother's womb.

He put together the right combination of genes to make you who you are. The Psalmist said that God *"knit him together."* The King James uses the phrase *"curiously wrought"* which actually means *"wrought with care."* A literal rendering would be, *"woven or embroidered with threads of different colors."* God only made one of you. The world will never see another just like you. God's originals are all masterpieces and can never be duplicated. God designed your personality, your appearance and your experiences to make you the special person He wants you to be.

This in no way justifies or excuses bad actions. Do not confuse the disappointment you feel because of your sinful nature with your worth as a person made in the image of God. Excluding the things you do in response to your sinful nature, whatever you do not like about yourself is a criticism of God's creative design. That would include such things as your height, race, speech, ancestry, personality and even your warts. The Psalmist said he was fearfully and wonderfully made. Do you feel the same way about yourself?

God knew all about you before you were born.

Nothing about you has ever surprised God. His eyes have been upon you since before you were born. And He has loved you since before you were born. There is a special line in a song written by Ronnie Hinson and Mike Payne that always thrills my soul. The song is called, *"When He Was On The Cross"* and the phrase that blesses me over and over is "He knew me, yet He loved me!" It is a waste of time to try to impress God. We try to impress others and hope that they do not see us at our bad moments, but God knows all about us and still loves us.

God ordered your days in advance.

Our God is so awesome that He knows the end from the beginning. He has so designed the world to allow us to have a choice and yet He knows exactly what is going to happen. The King James Bible translates verse 16 of Psalms 139 this way, *"all my members"* but the literal translation is *"all my days."* This verse says that God wrote the details of your life in His book before you had lived even a day! Beloved, God has planned or ordained your days in advance. You are where you are today because God is working out His special plan in your life. It would be profitable for you to find what God is doing, agree with His plan, and cooperate with Him to the best of your ability to see His plan completed.

God's thoughts and presence are with you continually.

When someone says to you "I was thinking about you the other day," it usually makes you feel special. It probably means they have not thought about you in a while, but something happened to bring you to their mind. That is good to know, but how much better to hear, "I think about you all the time." This is what David is saying about God. There is no way David can count all of God's thoughts toward him. God had Jeremiah tell Israel that His thoughts toward them are good, they are thoughts of peace and they are for a purpose and a pleasant ending (Jeremiah 29:11).

Not only are God's thoughts always with you, His presence is always with you. Through the years, Diane and I have often had one or more of our five grandsons spend the night with us. The two older boys are now in their teens and have outgrown spending the night with us. But the three younger ones still love to sleep over with Nanny and Poppy. Many times one will be afraid of the dark and Diane will lay down with him to get him to sleep. She tries to return to our room, but many times is awakened again by his frightened cries. What David is saying in verse 18 is—whether he is awake or asleep, God's presence is with him. He goes on to say in the rest of the Psalm that no matter where he goes, God will be with him.

Our thoughts should ever stay on this God who has us in His thoughts.

God made you.

God knows you.

God loves you.

Do you praise God for making you like you are?

Do you honor Him by being yourself and by using your special personality to glorify Him?

I am working on a book that God has put on my heart dealing with the subject of "the freedom to be you." I hope to have it finished soon and I believe and trust it will be helpful. I am trusting God to use it for His glory.

Chapter 11

Guarding Against Becoming the Lone Ranger

Bivocational pastors are busy people. If they are invited to attend a special conference or retreat, they will usually say they cannot because they do not have time. There is no denying that their schedules are maxed out. But, most of us can usually find the time to do the things we really want to do.

When I first began working with bivocational pastors in Tennessee, most associational Directors of Missions had this to say about the bivo pastors in their associations, "We do not know how to relate to or help our bivocational pastors. They will not come to any of our meetings." One reason they could not attend was that most meetings were held during hours the bivocational pastor had to be on his day job.

As I have worked with bivocational pastors over the years, I have discovered a few things about them:

- They need fellowship, encouragement, additional training and resources.

- They will come to meetings if someone personally recruits them.

- They respond best to one of their peers.

- The event must be practical and meet a need. If you strike out, they will not be back.

- They will have to give up something else to attend.

- Annual events need to be kept in the same time frame in order for them to schedule time away from work.

- Have something special for their wives so they can attend together.

- If they are helped and blessed they will be back.

Since bivocational pastors tend to be loners, we need to understand the factors which contribute to many becoming a "lone ranger."

Factors Which Lead to Isolation

A busy schedule

There is no doubt that a bivo pastor has a busy schedule. Many bivo pastors are busy studying or working when most of us are sleeping. Their day starts early and ends late. When asked to attend some event, even something he believes will be helpful, he already feels he is over scheduled. He is accustomed to being alone and he may even prefer being alone.

Physical fatigue

The result of having a very busy schedule and working long hours is fatigue. Burnout is a serious danger in the lives of many bivo pastors. They would do well to take our Lord's admonition to heart when He said to His disciples; *"Come ye yourselves apart into a desert place, and rest a while…"* (Mark 6:31).

Emotional exhaustion

Physical exhaustion can lead to emotional exhaustion. Emotional exhaustion can lead to depression. Depressed people usually want to be alone. It takes emotional energy to interact with others. Most bivo pastors would never admit they are depressed— they just push themselves to work harder.

Feelings of inadequacy or inferiority

While public opinion about bivocational pastors is improving, most bivo pastors have experienced critical remarks and putdowns from the ranks of fully-funded pastors. Some bivocational pastors do not have Bible College or seminary degrees. He hears how the mega churches are growing and sees himself as inadequate.

Living in survival mode

If you were to ask many bivocational pastors "How are you doing?" And, if they were honest most would have to say, "I am just trying to get by." Pastors who are trying to survive find it hard to force themselves to get out of the rut they are in.

Listening to the enemy who wants them isolated

We have a real enemy— Satan. Satan is the Destroyer whose basic strategy is to isolate and conquer. We are more vulnerable to Satan's attack when we are alone. He knows there is strength in numbers. He does not want us to go where we can be encouraged, blessed, strengthened and challenged.

Reasons to Spend Time with Other Pastors

1. **We need each other**

   God made us social creatures. *"It is not good for man to be alone"* applies to more than just marriage. I may be down today and you pick me up. You may be down tomorrow and I can pick you up. Solomon tells us in Proverbs 17:17, *"Iron sharpeneth iron, so a man sharpeneth the countenance of his friend."* Paul says in II Corinthians 1:3-7 that God comforts us so we can comfort others. I often tell a brother in Christ that I am a better man because God put him in my life. That is God's plan.

2. **We realize we are not alone**

   Being around other pastors and their wives who have gone through what we are going through helps us realize

we are not alone. Others have similar trials and testings. Satan tries to convince us that we are failures and
not worthy to be called a pastor. It always comes as a
surprise when a bivocational pastor discovers that there
are more like him, than those who are fully-funded.

3.   **We need to be refreshed**

Bivo pastors can become weary in the work we do. We
do not become weary of well-doing—but weary in well-
doing. There is something refreshing about being in the
presence of brothers and sisters in Christ. Paul often
talked about how we refresh one another.

> *"So that by God's will I may come to you
> with joy and together with you be refreshed"*
> (Romans 15:32 NIV).

> *"For they refreshed my spirit and yours also.
> Such men deserve recognition"* (I Corinthians
> 16:18 NIV).

> *"By all this we are encouraged"* (II Corin-
> thians 7:13 NIV).

> *"May the Lord show mercy to the household
> of Onesiphorus, because he often refreshed
> me and was not ashamed of my chains"* (II
> Timothy 1:16 NIV).

> *"Your love has given me great joy and encour-
> agement, because you, brother, have refreshed
> the hearts of the saints"* (Philemon 1:7).

4. **Our wives need an outlet**

I believe the most difficult role in the church is that of pastor's wife. There are many factors that produce loneliness and stress for the pastor's wife. Time pressure is probably the number one challenge for clergy marriages—not enough quality time together. Many times pastors' wives have few social outlets—apart from the church. They feel they cannot share with other women in the church, so when pressures build many times they have no one with whom to "vent," as my daughters call it. It is amazing to see how liberating it is for these pastors' wives to come to events designed especially for them and share with their peers.

5. **We get to share our stories, challenges and sermon ideas**

I have led retreats and conferences for bivo pastors and their wives for many years. They always enjoy the sessions led by the trained conference leaders, but I am amazed that some of the most productive interaction comes during break time or meals. They learn so much from the interaction with each other. Also, lasting friendships are born during these gatherings.

Ways to Connect

1. **Get involved in your local association**

The best way to make a connection is to get involved with fellow pastors in your local association. When your schedule permits, attend pastors' conferences and fellowship events so you can get to know fellow pastors. You will find one or more guys who have a kindred spirit. That is a relationship worth developing. The first step to getting involved with others can be taken in your own community where time and distance are the least prohibitive.

2.   **Seek a friend and prayer partner**

Everyone needs a best friend. Your mother probably told you "to have a friend you must be a friend." Well, that is still true. There is probably a pastor near you who could use a friend. Those of us who have been in the ministry for a long time can attest to the fact that it was a special friend who helped us make it through difficult times. You need that guy who will pick up the phone, drop what he's doing and listen to you without being judgmental and weep or laugh with you through whatever you are facing.

3.   **Attend bivocational retreats and events in your area**

It has been rewarding to watch bivo pastors and their wives come alive with excitement at our retreats. For many, the first thing added to their calendar each year is the bivocational ministers and wives retreat. God never fails to meet needs. Many have come to the retreat intending to resign from their church when they return home. They often email me afterward to say they went back with a new determination to stay in the battle.

God has chosen to bless and use events such as this to strengthen the commitment of His servants.

4. Stay connected through our website

The website for the Bivocational and Small Church Leadership Network (BivoSmallChurch.net) is loaded with helpful articles and resources. You will discover a world of information and sermon outlines which will enrich your ministry. Upcoming events and opportunities are posted on a regular basis so that you can stay informed on what's coming in the future.

5. Ask someone you admire to mentor you

I am thankful for the great men of God who cared and took the time to mentor me. It is encouraging to discover that many are willing to give of themselves to help you learn some of the things God has taught them. I know from personal experience they gain tremendously from the relationship. There may be someone you admire who would be eager to walk with you over the next months or years. My pastor took me under his wing when I was nineteen years old and walked with me until I was well in my twenties. There have been others whom God brought into my life during the early years of my ministry. Why not get up the courage to ask? It may prove to be one of the wisest decisions you will ever make.

6. **Find a young preacher and become his friend and encourager**

The dropout rate among young ministers is alarming. These young men heard the call of God and responded. Some have spent several years preparing. They all will need a helping hand at some point. Do you know a young minister who could use some encouragement? It may be your support that helps him develop his full potential. Helping young ministers to weather some of the storms I have gone through is one of the driving forces in my life. If I can be used to help just one young man in the same way God allowed others to help me, I feel my journey will have had a measure of success.

Chapter 12

How Much is a Bivocational Pastor Worth?

One of the most frequently asked questions I get from churches and a pastor search committee is "What should we pay a bivocational pastor?" First I tell them to check the *Compensation Study* provided on the website of most state conventions. The survey usually includes the size of the congregation, the annual budget income and whether the pastor is bivocational or fully-funded. What other churches are paying their pastor is only one factor contributing to the worth of a pastor to his church, whether he is bivocational or fully-funded.

A bivocational pastor is not a "part-time" pastor.

A bivocational pastor is not a "little preacher."

A bivocational pastor is not a "second-class preacher."

He may not receive a full time salary from the church, but he is the pastor of the church all day—every day. As stated earlier in a previous chapter, a faithful pastor is worthy of double honor.

> *"Let the elders that rule well be counted worthy of double honor, especially they who labour in the word and doctrine. For the scripture saith; Thou shalt not muzzle the ox that treadeth out the corn. And the labourer is worthy of his reward"* (I Timothy 5:17, 18).

Strong's Concordance defines the word translated "honour" as "money paid." This suggests that a Biblically sound pastor should receive extra compensation. This passage also includes the encouragement to hold a faithful pastor in honor or high esteem.

Today the office of pastor no longer holds the respect of the community that it once did. The few high profile preachers who have had a moral failure have produced distaste and distrust for the position of pastor.

Most church members have no appreciation for the demands and pressures placed on their pastor on a daily basis. The Apostle Paul made it known that caring for the needs of churches is a special challenge for the man of God when he said, *"Beside those things that are without, that which cometh upon me daily, the care of all the churches"* (II Corinthians 11:28).

Only a pastor fully understands when a fellow pastor describes the pressures of the pastorate. This is why the pastor reacts when he hears someone say, "A pastor only works three hours a week." A God-called, Spirit-filled, Bible preaching, people loving shepherd is priceless. When a church has such a pastor it should do everything it can to support, follow, encourage and adequately pay the man God sent them.

A God-called shepherd is not a hireling who flees when the wolf comes (John 10:11-14). He cares for the sheep and lays down his life for the wellbeing of the flock. People need to understand that the pastor is not "their" minister, but Christ's minister for them. This is how the Apostle Paul identifies the pastor of the church at Colosse (Colossians 1:7). He gets his orders from God and will one day give an answer to God for how he led that church.

There is a Biblical mandate for individuals to respect and support God's chosen people, especially their leaders. *"He suffered no man to do them wrong; yea, he reproved kings for their sake, saying. Touch not mine anointed, and do my prophets no harm"* (I Chronicles 16:21, 22). If there is any doubt that God means what He says— talk to the sister of Moses, Miriam (Numbers 12:1-15) and Korah and his family (Numbers 16:1-35).

To fully understand the worth of a faithful pastor, talk to that church which has been without a pastor for two or three years or that church which has had two or three bad experiences with undesirable pastors. Years ago the term "Man of God" had real significance in most communities. I have heard people say, "Preachers are a dime a dozen!" I assure you that real men of God are not.

The pressure of being on call twenty-four hours a day, seven days a week takes its toll on the average pastor. I cannot count all the times I have been called back from vacation or other family event to preach a funeral or help in a crisis. People do not always die or face a major crisis from 9am to 5pm Monday through Friday.

Pastoring a church where there are many needs takes a lot of emotional energy. It is actually like being on the front lines of a spiritual war. Regular periods of R & R are essential. For fourteen years I was pastor of an inner city church with a lot of older adults. For the first five or six years I spent most of my time visiting the hospitals or the funeral homes. I found that I had to get out of the city for at least one night every month. That was the only way I could get refreshed and recharged to go back in the battle.

One of the mistakes made by churches that have a bivocational pastor is to think they should pay him based on what he is making at his other job. The thought is that he is already making enough money to provide for his family so the church does not need to pay him much. That is penalizing him for being willing to work another job to help provide for his family while pastoring their church. A bivocational pastor's salary should be based on the churches ability to pay. What he makes at his second job should not be a factor! If he chooses to take less than what the church is willing and able to pay, that is his decision.

Remember, because he has two full-time jobs, his free time will be limited. Therefore, he may have to hire someone to do some things that he would otherwise be doing; such as, mowing the grass and performing handyman jobs around the house. This does not mean that he is too important to do such tasks. It simply means he does not have the time or energy to do these things. He is giving priority to the major things he must get done.

The bivocational pastor has so much on him that he should not have to deal with financial pressure if it can be helped. However, this does not excuse poor money management on his part. A church often finds that if they are blessing their pastor financially, he is often blessing others who are less fortunate.

The family of the bivocational pastor almost always sees less of him than they would like. The church should insist that he and his family take a real vacation at least once a year. Going to visit parents or grandparents does not qualify as a vacation. A real vacation takes extra money. The church should see that he has vacation time and vacation pay. As a result they will by having a healthier and happier pastor.

Acts of appreciation throughout the year will endear the congregation to their pastor and his family. These need not always be in the form of money. A new suit, tickets to a special event, a gift card shower, free babysitting if needed or a special day to honor the pastor or his wife are just a few suggestions.

History is replete with examples of men of God who have been unappreciated and mistreated whether it is the faithful prophets in the Old Testament, the early church martyrs or the many dedicated pastors today. Pity the church that is guilty of mistreating the man of God or his family.

Whether or not a bivocational pastor is rewarded according to his true worth in this life, Almighty God will reward all faithful pastors with a crown of glory on the payday that really counts. *"And when the chief Shepherd shall appear, ye shall receive a crown of glory that fadeth not away"* (I Peter 5:4).

Chapter 13

The Bivocational Pastor's Family

The number one issue for bivocational pastors is time management. The number one failure of bivocational pastors is short changing the family. This is not his plan. He simply ends up neglecting them by default. He runs out of time before he gets to do what he should with his family. Therefore, it is imperative that he develop some strategies which put his family in the rightful place they deserve in his life.

I still remember quite vividly a bivo pastor sharing with a group of his peers several years ago how his son got his attention. Since that brother is now in heaven, I will allow him to remain anonymous. He told about coming home one night after a busy day at work. He was in his recliner studying, when his 10 year old son tried to get his attention. He told his son to leave him alone; he was too busy to be interrupted. After several unsuccessful attempts to talk to his dad, he stomped out of the room and said, "I wish I was one of your members; maybe then you would talk to me." He said that got his attention.

How many other children of bivo pastors say the same thing?

One of the most pressing motivations in my life today is to help young ministers not make some of the same mistakes I made when I started pastoring. I remember with remorse how I would often leave my young wife and three small children home at night while I went out again to do my "ministry." Some weeks I would spend most of forty hours just visiting members in the hospitals. My children would grab my legs and beg me to stay home with them. My wife came close to having a nervous breakdown. I was sincere, but I was sincerely wrong!

I realized later that I needed the accolades of others to boost my weak self-identity. It was truly a liberating day when I discovered that my real-identity was based on who God says I am—not on who others think I am. I plan for that to be the subject of my next book.

Years ago, as I was leading a conference on bivocational ministry in Knoxville, Tennessee, a young lady talked to me during a break. She told me she was engaged to be married soon to a young preacher. She said she had been given some advice by an older minister which disturbed her. He had told her that she needed to get accustomed to the fact that her husband would be "married" to the church he pastored. She was disturbed and wanted to know if this was right. I assured her that it was not right. I said, "You will be his bride. The church is the bride of Christ!"

Many a young pastor makes the serious mistake of concluding that his devotion to God places the church above his family. God and the church are not one and the same. God does come before anyone or anything else in your life, including your family. The church does not. If a minister loses one church, there is a good possibility he will get another. If he loses his family, he most likely will not get another church.

I have discovered that most churches appreciate it when their pastor gives his wife and children preferential treatment. They like to see their pastor committed to his family. If they do not like it, do it anyway. It is their loss.

We should never forget that God instituted the family long before He instituted the church. The family unit is the basic building block of an orderly society. Strong families make strong churches.

The church is in desperate need of good family models. It is commonly reported that the divorce rate among church goers is just as high as none church goers. Pastors should lead their churches to make building healthy families a priority. If we decide to do so, we will probably be embarrassed to discover the fact that most church activities separate families instead of bringing them together.

We intentionally have "family fun night" at our church. Family fun night is a Sunday night regularly set aside for fun and fellowship for the entire family. It builds families, gives a good outing to young families and teaches our children that Christians know how to have fun. It is a great opportunity to attract prospective young families. It helps anchor most of the social life of your children and teens around the church.

One of the best things you can show your church is how much you love your wife. You can set the example for the men in your church on how to treat their wives. It is not easy being a pastor's wife. She is often taken for granted, waits quietly in the shadows while you receive generous applause and loves you in spite of seeing all your warts. Why not acknowledge your appreciation for her advice and support before the congregation? This will also help to deter any advances from a woman in the church who may have an unhealthy attraction to you.

It is easy for a busy bivo pastor to begin taking his wife for granted. This was certainly true in my case. In the early years of ministry, I never stopped to notice how desperately my wife needed my help and support around the house. God began to burn a special verse into my heart. That verse is I Peter 3:7.

> *"Likewise, ye husbands, dwell with them according to the knowledge, giving honor unto the wife, as unto the weaker vessel, and as being heirs together of the grace of life; that your prayers be not hindered."*

I had become an expert on the first six verses of that chapter. It deals with how the wife is to treat her husband. The Lord convinced me that those verses were none of my business. That was between Him and my wife! He told me to concentrate on verse 7. That verse helped me to realize I was to become a life-long student of my wife. I am to know her better than she knows herself. I am to learn her weaknesses, her strengths, her fears, her basic needs of spiritual leadership, communication, affection and commitment, her moods, her love language and her giftedness. I am to give honor to her by placing her above other people and things; by showing her she is special, by serving her, by valuing her opinion, by spending time with her, by protecting her and by making her my best friend.

I learned from that verse that we are heirs together of God's grace for living. That verse teaches that my best shot at life is with her as my partner. Finally, verse 7 let me know that a poor relationship with my wife would hinder both of us from getting answers to prayers. If God allows me a few more productive years, I plan to put the results of that study in book form.

The last thing a pastor wants to do is win his community but lose his family. A helpful guideline to keep that from happening is to always be who you are at home, in public and behind the pulpit. If your wife and children believe you are a hypocrite, your primary ministry has already become ineffective. Never place undue pressure on your wife and children to make you look good. If they do not naturally appreciate and acknowledge your honesty, sincerity, trustworthiness, transparency and goodness, you are already in trouble.

Why do some preacher's kids turn out to be rebels while others follow in the footsteps of their parents in a life of ministry? Each situation is unique, but generally speaking, kids rebel against hypocrisy (dad is one thing at home and something else at church), against excessive discipline (where kids are punished too severely for misconduct) and against a legalistic code which takes the fun out of life (kids are never allowed to be like other kids).

I was saved and called to preach in a very legalistic church. I was unusually zealous and held rigid standards of outward evidence of godliness. I refused to have a television in our home. My wife and girls were not allowed to wear shorts or even long pants. Slowly, God began to convict me of my hypocrisy.

For instance, I would go to a friend's house to watch a ball-game I wanted to see. Also, when we took our youth on a hayride, I insisted that the girls wear dresses or skirts. As they climbed a step ladder to get in the trailer for the hayride, very little was left to the imagination of the boys on the ground. At that occasion, a dress or skirt was not modest apparel! Also, I soon became aware that a dress can be very immodest if it was too tight, too low cut or too short.

God sent me to pastor a very legalistic church on the back-side of the desert in Mississippi. There, He delivered me from legalism and taught me to love people. Then, He put me back into His Kingdom work.

We often hear comments about the difficulty of growing up in a preacher's home. While I will not minimize the struggles a preacher's children face, I believe it is time to highlight the advantages of being a PK. Although, I am sure not every pastor's home is what it should be, there is a very good possibility that the following statements are true in most pastors' homes. For every one you show me which are not what they should be, I will show ten who are.

1. In a pastor's home, you get to be around great men and women of God who visit, preach and teach in your church.

2. You will be raised in a home where the Bible is the guide book for life.

3. You will have a family that believes and lives by the moral code of the Ten Commandments.

4. You will get to witness the benefits of honoring God in your home.

5. You are much less likely to be the product of a broken home.

6. You will have a good probability of coming to know the Lord at an early age.

7. You can claim the blessings God promises to those who know and serve Him. Psalms 37:25-28, Proverbs 11:18-21; Isaiah 61:9.

Here are a few concluding suggestions on giving your family their rightful place in your busy schedule.

■   Try to maintain a date night with your wife. Use your imagination to create special ways to make that happen.

■   Once a month, date your daughters and take your sons on outings. In doing so, you will develop memories each of you will cherish.

■   Be sure and place family special days on your calendar. This includes birthdays, anniversaries, graduations, ballgames, vacations, reunions and special outings. If you have a date with your daughter on your calendar, when someone calls to get you to do something, you can rightfully say "I am sorry but I already have an important event scheduled at that time!" You do not even owe it to them to tell them what you have planned. Your daughter's appreciation will last a lot longer than their disappointment.

There is much more which could be discussed regarding the bivo pastor's family. However, there is enough in this chapter to give you encouragement to make the adjustments necessary for your family to thank God you are their leader.

Chapter 14

Receiving & Sharing a Word from the Lord

How many people will go to bed hungry tonight? Famine is a serious concern in many parts of the world today. Our hearts should go out to all those who would love to have a good meal before they go to bed. There is another famine in the land which has more severe consequence than the first. This is a famine of hearing the Word of God. The Prophet Amos predicted these days centuries ago.

> *"Behold, the days come, saith the Lord God, that I will send a famine in the land, not a famine of bread, nor a*

thirst for water, but of hearing the words of the Lord"
(Amos 8:11).

Today there is too much preaching of man's opinion and not God's Word. Listen to Jeremiah's words.

> *"The prophet that hath a dream, let him tell a dream; and he that hath my word, let him speak my word faithfully. What is the chaff to the wheat? Saith the Lord. Is not my word like a fire? Saith the Lord; and like a hammer that breaketh the rock in pieces?"* (Jeremiah 23:28-29).

There was a time when Jeremiah got discouraged and decided that he would quit preaching. However, he found that he could not keep silent. *"Then I said I will not make mention of him, nor speak any more in his name. But his word was in my heart as a burning fire shut up in my bones, and I was weary with forbearing and I could not stay"* (Jeremiah 20:9). All God called preachers need to know how to receive and share a word from the Lord. In this chapter we will discuss ways to help that happen.

Demonstrate the Power of a Call from God

To be called of God to speak to his generation is one of the greatest honors to be placed upon any man. It is a humbling yet exciting challenge. God's servants have been called to deliver a message not preach a sermon. The Spirit of God anoints and empowers God's messengers. The Prophet Ezekiel said this should happen when God's man speaks. *"And when this cometh to pass, (lo, it will come) then shall they know that a prophet hath been among them"* (Ezekiel 33:33).

The call to speak for God is not something one can ignore or neglect without serious consequences. The Apostle Paul went so far as to say *"Woe is me if I preach not the Gospel"* (I Corinthians 9:16-17). God has a message He wants presented to a sinful world. The one called to deliver the message has been given a great honor and an awesome responsibility. Every Christian is called to be a witness for Christ. However, no one should attempt to pastor a church and become its primary preacher without a call of God to do so. Those who choose to do so on their own usually do not stay in the ministry.

Depend on the Authority of the Word of God

There is no authority greater than the Word of God. We do not need to defend it; we just need to present it. Even when people say they do not believe it; give it to them any way. The Word of God is the Sword of the Spirit. There is no need to tell someone the effort used to sharpen the sword, just stick him with it. He will get the point! The prophets of old were powerful when they said, *"Thus saith the Lord"* or when they wrote *"The Word of the Lord came to the prophet."*

Get the Message for the Hour

It is much more rewarding to have something to say than to have to say something! God's Word is a living book and it relates to where we are and what we are facing today. The serious student of the Word of God knows that when he reads the Word it starts reading him. The Spirit of God takes timeless principles recorded in the Bible and begins to apply them to our lives and circumstances. The Apostles often made application by saying what Peter said in Acts 2:16, "But this is that which was spoken by the prophet Joel." The classic example is found in Luke 4:16-21, when our Lord entered the synagogue in Nazareth and was asked to speak. The book of Isaiah was handed to Him; He opened the book and found the place where it was written. He read the text, sat down and said *"This day is this scripture fulfilled in your ears."* The most serious search for all men of God is the search for the message for the hour.

Prepare Body, Mind and Heart to Preach

A preacher should get as much rest as possible before he is to preach. It is amazing the things which come up on most Saturdays to keep a pastor from preparing himself to deliver God's Word the next day. It is also common for major distractions to occur just before the time he is to go to the pulpit to preach. Therefore, preachers need to realize this is one of the strategies of the enemy and he must refuse to let him take the message from his heart. Most pastors can tell stories about the many disturbing things he was told about his church or one of his members just before he entered the pulpit to preach. The preacher should saturate his mind with the message for as long as possible just before he gets up to preach.

Walk into the Pulpit Pure, Prayed-Up and Prepared

The Spirit of God will not fill and use a dirty vessel. The Prophet Isaiah said it well when he said: *"Be ye clean that bear the vessels of the Lord*" (Isaiah 52:11). No preacher should ever enter the pulpit with known sin in his life.

Before he talks to people about God, he should spend time talking to God about the people to whom he will speak. The preacher's heart should be tempered by the serious word he is about to share and by the love he has for his people. A good question to ask before beginning to preach is: "Have I prayed about what I am planning to say?"

Nothing takes the place of serious study when it comes to sermon preparation. The preacher is about to ask a congregation to give him thirty to forty-five minutes of their time. What he shares should be well constructed, interesting and worth the time they will invest.

Seek and Speak in the Power of the Holy Spirit

It is essential that the man of God be filled with the Holy Spirit. Only the Spirit of God can take the Word of God and change a life. Man's best efforts can only produce surface corrections. While a certain level of education is helpful, the most important factor is the anointing of the Holy Spirit. Even a man with limited education and communication skills can become extremely effective when he is filled with the Holy Spirit. An older preacher was asked what kind of preacher he was, he replied, "I am a pretty good preacher if my Partner shows up!"

In seeking the direction and power of the Holy Spirit the man of God must be willing to do whatever the Spirit leads him to do. This means he will probably be led out of his comfort zone. One thing he learns as he allows the Spirit to use him is that he can trust the Holy Spirit to know what He is doing and how to accomplish the will and purposes of God.

Speak in Plain, Simple Terms

The primary purpose of preaching is to influence those who are listening. A preacher is wasting his time and that of his congregation if they do not comprehend his message.

When a preacher has finished speaking, the question should never be "What did he say?" but it should be "What am I going to do with what he said?"

Jesus Christ is our best model for speaking so that everyone knows what is being said. The scripture says that *"the common people heard Him gladly"* (Mark 12:37). His illustrations came from everyday life. Those who had trouble understanding were those who would not accept the truth but had a predisposed opinion of what they wanted to believe.

The Apostle Paul clearly admonishes us in Ephesians 4:15 *"speak the truth in love."* People need to hear the truth in as plain and simple terms as one can use. This was verified in a conversation I had with a lady after I finished preaching several years ago. She told me that I spoke like everyone in the congregation was in the fifth grade. Then she said that was a good thing because now she could understand me.

My response was that I spoke that way for two reasons. One, I am a simple man and I have no desire to be complicated when I speak. Second, my goal is to speak so clearly that no one misunderstands.

Speak Heart to Heart

Preachers should never preach to impress the minds of their hearers but to touch their hearts. When Peter preached on the day of Pentecost, those who heard him *"were pricked in their heart"* (Acts 2:37). Therefore, it is important for a preacher to know that if his message does not stir him it most likely will not stir others.

As I have listened to some men preach, I wondered if they really believed what they were saying. Speaking without passion and conviction will cause others to wonder the same thing. Even though they may not agree with you, your audience wants to believe you really mean what you are saying.

Years ago I read a novel written by George McDonald entitled, *The Curate's Awakening*, that impressed me significantly. A curate is someone we would call today an apprentice preacher. This young man was preaching in a church in Scotland where he was confronted by an agnostic. The agnostic told him plainly that he did not think the young preacher believed a thing he had said. This so disturbed the young preacher that it led him to do some serious soul-searching. The search ultimately resulted in the young preacher's true conversion.[3]

Use Proper Body Language

There is more to what you are saying than just what comes out of your mouth. Words are extremely important. But, how we say what we say is also important. According to communications expert, Albert Mehrabian, seven percent of what we communicate

---

[3] McDonald, George, Hurst & Blackett Publishers, 1876, London, Bethany House Publishers, 1985 Minneapolis, Minnesota p.24

is done through words, thirty-eight percent is done through tone and fifty-five percent is done through body language.[4] Whether we agree with his percentages or not, we must agree that body language is important. We have all heard the story about the little boy who was sitting on the front row listening to the preacher. As the speaker, who was using a corded mike, shouted and moved from side to side, he leaned over to his mother and said, "Mommy, what will he do if he gets loose?"

A preacher's body language communicates long before he stands up to speak. Does he carry himself with an air of superiority? Does he participate in the singing? Does he acknowledge the people around him? Does he appear impatient to start speaking? Is he dressed extravagantly? All of these speak volumes.

When he begins to speak, the preacher should watch his posture and nervous mannerisms. He should hold himself erect. He should not slump over the pulpit. He should keep his hands away from his mouth when he is speaking. He should not focus over the heads of the congregation or look from corner to corner. He should make eye contact with the congregation. The eye is the window of the soul. I never trust a man who refuses to look me in the eye when we are talking.

Vary the Rate of Speech and Voice Pitch

Most people find it hard to concentrate if the preacher speaks in a monotone even if the content is interesting. A preacher must learn to get excited, be serious, get loud or soft, talk fast or deliberate as the message dictates. A young preacher is usually consumed

---

4 Mehrabian, A., (1981) Silent Message: Implicit Communication of Emotions and Attitudes, Belmont, CA. Wadsworth

by what he is saying. As he becomes more experienced, he will be equally concerned about how he is saying it. When a preacher has his message on his heart and not just in his head, how he says it will come naturally if he allows himself to speak freely.

There are those who start out loud and stay loud. This can be equally frustrating for the congregation. In some areas of the country, the quality of a preacher's sermon is judged by how loud he speaks, how hoarse he is when he finishes and how profusely he perspired. People need to realize that is a cultural issue and not a spiritual issue. Effectiveness should be the goal and not style. However, every preacher should guard against doing what one did when he wrote in his notes, "Holler loud, this is a weak point!"

Give Special Attention to the Introduction

A preacher should give special attention to the introduction to his message. He will either gain the attention or lose his audience within the first three minutes of his message. The worse thing he can do is stumble around verbally as he starts. Therefore, a few guidelines will help insure that his message has a good beginning. For one thing he should tell the congregation where he is going in his sermon.

Years ago someone gave me a simple plan for sermon development: "Tell them what you are going to say, say it and then, remind them of what you said!" The introduction should be developed in detail. Every word should be chosen carefully. It should be as clear and forceful as it can possibly be. Then, it should be written down in the sermon notes just as it is to be presented. The importance of the introduction cannot be overstated.

Develop a Comfortable Outline

The order in which the message is presented is vitally important. There should be a comfortable flow to the development of the message. Some preachers choose to write out their sermon just like they plan to preach it. Usually, I develop an outline which helps me stay on track. I place my main points in the order they are to be presented. Then, for easy recall I select a key word or phrase for each point. Last, I place three or more sub-points under each main point for developing the message. There should be enough information in the outline for you to pick up the outline later and preach it again without forgetting most of the content. Any message, worth preaching is worth preaching again if you work on it to fit the current situation.

Always Apply the Message to the Audience

After giving a preacher thirty to forty-five minutes of their time a congregation has a right to ask, "So what?" They want to know what they are expected to do as a result of the message. I have always written out a few concluding statements which challenges the congregation to respond in specific ways. We should draw the net carefully. The response to the message is left up to each individual but no one should leave the worship service wondering how the message applies to him.

Know When to Finish

The effectiveness of many sermons has often been nullified because the speaker did not know when to quit. Sometimes he will repeat himself over and over or "chase rabbits" instead of drawing the message to a proper conclusion. As a young preacher, I was told, "Stand up, speak up and shut up!" It is an unusual preacher who can hold an audience's attention over thirty-five to forty minutes. I often begin speaking by telling a humorous story. An old preacher got up to preach and said, "I understand that it is my job to preach and your job to listen. If you get through before I do, let me know!"

A Preacher Should Do His Best and Leave the Rest to God

The immediate outward results of a message are not the defining evaluation of the message. We can only see the outward results. God sees the heart. We see the short term effect. God measures the eternal dividends. There have been times when I felt like I had done a miserable job, but later learned that God had changed a life. The only score keeping that matters is kept in heaven. The real payday for the man of God is when our Lord says, *"Well done, good and faithful servant!"*

Chapter 15

Should a Bivocational Pastor Become Fully-Funded?

Many bivocational pastors dream of the day they can quit their second job and become fully-funded pastors. There are others who refuse to become fully-funded even though their church can afford to pay them a full salary. Moving from bivo status to fully-funded should not be viewed as the natural step of advancement in the ministry. Every situation is different. Some pastors actually function better in a bivocational role. If a church grows to the point where funds are available to pay the pastor a salary which would adequately provide for his family, it is perfectly acceptable for him to stop his other job and become fully-funded. However, it is also acceptable for him to remain bivocational and use the extra income to invest in sharing the Gospel at home and abroad. Also the pastor may feel that it is God's plan for him to remain bivocational regardless of the income of the church.

A pastor should not consider himself fully-funded unless the salary and benefits he receives provides adequately for the needs of his family. The church should allow its pastor to take on extra work if the salary it pays is not sufficient. It is embarrassing the salary some pastors are expected to live on.

I recently spoke with a pastor whose entire compensation from his church was about twenty-three thousand dollars. He and his wife had six children. She was on disability and received a monthly check just under one thousand dollars. They were receiving two hundred dollars a month in food stamps and had medical insurance with the state. She received a twenty-nine dollar a month cost of living increase. The meager increase to her monthly check meant she made too much to continue receiving food stamps and insurance. He asked the church to allow him to take a second job. They refused, saying it would not look good if their pastor had to go to work! I told him to take care of his family first. If the church could not agree to that decision, then they could find another pastor and God would lead him to another church which would honor his commitment to his family.

A few years ago I spoke with a pastor who had been given a salary increase by his church. He was so excited as he told me he had quit his second job to become fully-funded at the church. He said he was going to try it for a few months to see if they could make it without his second income. I will always remember his final remark. He said if it did not work out, his wife could go to work! I gently rebuked him by saying,"There is a more honorable solution. You can go back to work."

I have discovered that we usually rise to the level of the challenges we face. Most bivo pastors, of necessity have learned to work at a fast pace. Becoming fully-funded does not automatically produce an abundance of extra time.

I was told by a bivo pastor who had finally been able to quit his second job to become fully-funded at the church that he was surprised to discover how little extra time he really had after the move. He found he added other things to his daily routine which he had not had time to do before.

If a bivo pastor is blessed to be able to quit his second job and focus solely on being a pastor, he should not think or act like he has arrived. The real key to success as a pastor is to be faithful where God has put you and let Him move you as He chooses.

Chapter 16

Conclusion—
Enjoy the Journey

What an awesome privilege to be called of God to preach His Word and to be the shepherd of a local flock! Too often pastors find themselves focusing on external things such as the size of the flock, the size of the building and the size of the paycheck instead of the wonder of being on assignment with God. The amazing thing is God is willing to call and use any of us!

Does this call of God include hardships, testings and trials? Of course it does. We are called to model our lives after our Lord Jesus Christ. We are in the caravan of faith which includes all who have answered the call since our forefather, Abraham, responded to God's call centuries ago. Many have faithfully completed their journey. It is our time to benefit from the witness of those who have gone before, focus on our Model, Jesus Christ, and joyfully anticipate the fruit of our labors and the home that awaits us. The writer of Hebrews said it like this:

> *"Wherefore seeing we also are compassed about with so great a cloud of witnesses, let us lay aside every weight, and the sin which doth so easily beset us, and let us run with patience the race that is set before us, looking unto Jesus the author and finisher of our faith; who for the joy that was set before Him endured the cross, despising the shame, and is set down at the right hand of the throne of God"* (Hebrews 12:1-2).

A few years ago I had one of the most delightful days of my life. I had been invited to return to a church I had pastored for fourteen years. I was to preach the last sermon at the church before they closed their doors and gave the building to a new church start. Former members had received invitations to return for the last service. I was surprised to find several hundred people in attendance. Throughout the day I talked with people who reminded me of how I had helped them heal a broken marriage, or rescue a wayward son, or find new life in Christ, or discover God's will for their lives and find the joy of living for Christ.

The strange thing was that I had forgotten many of those experiences until I was reminded of them. It seemed that the Lord said to me, "This is a little taste of what heaven will be like!"

We are investing our lives in things with eternal dividends. The principle of investing over a long period of time has shown us that we earn much more than we invest as we reap the benefit of compounded interest.

This principle is true with spiritual investments as well. When we invest in the life of another, we will draw from the benefits of what he does for God. This is our spiritual tree which will be fully revealed in heaven. I believe the Lord will take each of His faithful servants by the hand and say to him, *"Come see what I have done with what you did for me!"* What a day that will be!

Enjoy the journey.

Appendix

Doing The Best With Your Pastor's Financial Support

by Richard Skidmore, Financial Support,
Tennessee Baptist Convention

Consider

S<u>cripture</u> teaches that ministers are to be paid in a manner worthy of their labor. Passages like Luke 10:7, I Corinthians 9:14, Galations 6:6 and I Timothy 5:17-18 give instructions for the church to provide well for their ministers.

<u>Stewardship</u> leads to *planning* compensation. Churches may be tempted to use the "package" approach. This will nearly always

unnecessarily increase the tax liability of the minister and thus cause him to have less money to provide for the needs of his family. Often this results in the payment of 25% or more in taxes that he may not legally owe. For instance, funds used for automobile expenses paid by the minister after money has been delivered to him in a package are subject to both federal income tax and SECA tax. A compensation plan that provides an accountable reimbursement plan for ministry expenses results in no tax payment on those dollars. Detailed expense reports give Personnel and Finance Committees a much clearer understanding of the ministry and expenses of their ministers.

Simplicity will flourish with a good compensation plan. Package amounts lead to confusion about what amount constitutes a minister's real income. Church members who see the package amount may not be aware that the package includes ministry-related expenses, the cost of medical insurance, retirement contributions, and the payment of the total social security tax by ministers. Their understanding will be greatly enhanced with the adoption of a good compensation plan.

Review

Written policies are vital in defining the compensation practices of the church. A variety of issues should be addressed in these documents. A clear plan for reimbursing ministry-related expenses should be in place. The church and minister need information that is easily understood as to the provision of benefits and personal income. Income policies should define how housing allowance is designated for the ministers of the church. Other matters that should be addressed include vacation, sick leave, sabbatical leave, work hours, pay periods, employee classifications, or other hiring issues.

Has the church maintained or adjusted income levels by granting cost of living increases? Who has the responsibility of personnel review and the recommendation of merit increases?

Receive

<u>Information</u> should be gathered regularly by the church as she seeks to treat her ministers well.

<u>Compensation studies</u> should be investigated. Most state conventions participate in a survey of churches to determine the amount of income and benefits provided to various church staff members. Contact your state convention for information.

Plan

Three separate areas will emerge in a good compensation plan.

<u>Ministry-related expenses</u> should be handled on an accountable reimbursement basis. These expenses should **NOT** be included in a "package" amount. They should not be paid as "allowances" which will increase the tax liability of the minister. They should be funded by the church in a line item separate from income.

<u>Protection coverage and benefits</u> should provide adequately for insurance and retirement. A medical insurance plan as well as life and disability insurance should be required components of protection for the minister and his family members. Retirement contributions should be made wisely. For a variety of reasons, retirement contributions should be placed in the Church Retirement Plan.

These factors include SECA tax considerations, housing benefits in retirement, and protection coverage provided by state conventions for ministers involved in the Church Retirement Plan. Your state convention or GuideStone Financial Resources of the Southern Baptist Convention can provide answers to your questions.

<u>Income</u> includes salary and, for ministers, the possibility of housing allowance and a Social Security offset. Be sure that housing allowance is clearly understood and utilized by your ministers. If there is any question for a staff minister other than the pastor as to whether that person should be treated as a minister for tax purposes, contact your state convention for assistance. It is vital to the financial support plan that this issue be clear.

Consult with those who clearly understand the special tax rules that apply to ministers and churches. IRS forms, reporting requirements, self-employment social security taxes, housing, and a variety of other issues make compensation planning for ministers and churches complex.